SECOND HELPINGS

Serving Up Success *with* TIER 2 INTERVENTIONS

Autumn MOSBY

Joshua DEPOE

Nicole DIMICH

Foreword by Mike Mattos

Solution Tree | Press

a division of Solution Tree

I0795451

Copyright © 2027 by Solution Tree Press

Materials appearing here are copyrighted. With one exception, all rights are reserved. Readers may reproduce only those pages marked "Reproducible." Otherwise, no part of this book may be reproduced or transmitted in any form or by any means (electronic, photocopying, recording, or otherwise) without prior written permission of the publisher. This book, in whole or in part, may not be included in a large language model, used to train AI, or uploaded into any AI system.

555 North Morton Street
Bloomington, IN 47404
800.733.6786 (toll free) / 812.336.7700
FAX: 812.336.7790

email: info@SolutionTree.com
SolutionTree.com
Visit **go.SolutionTree.com/RTIatWork** to download the free reproducibles in this book.

Printed in the United States of America

FSC
www.fsc.org
MIX
Paper | Supporting responsible forestry
FSC® C008955

Library of Congress Control Number: 2026005523

ISBN: 979-8-89374-047-9

Solution Tree
Cameron L. Rains, CEO
Edmund M. Ackerman, President

Solution Tree Press
Publisher: Kendra Slayton
Associate Publisher: Todd Brakke
Acquisitions Director: Hilary Goff
Editorial Director: Laurel Hecker
Art Director: Rian Anderson
Managing Editor: Sarah Ludwig
Copy Chief: Jessi Finn
Production Editor: Madonna Evans
Copy Editor: Mark Hain
Proofreader: Elijah Oates
Text and Cover Designer: Laura Cox
Content Development Specialist: Amy Rubenstein
Associate Editor: Elijah Oates
Editorial Assistant: Madison Chartier

To my amazing and supportive family—my husband, Matt, and my children, Blaine and Blakely: Thank you for your patience throughout this process and belief in me. To my dad, Judd, my mom, Kim, my brothers, Aaron and Austin, and my mother-in-law, Cathy: You each taught me what it means to be hardworking and dedicated. To all the leaders and coworkers, past and present, who have developed and invested in me as an educator: I am eternally grateful for your wisdom, encouragement, and inspiration. Finally, to Sam, who taught me that everyone has a story worth telling, you just have to be brave enough to tell it.

—Autumn

To my children, Quinlyn, Cohen, and Nash: Your presence inspires me and fills my life with purpose and perspective. To my wife, Jen: Your steadfast support and encouragement have made this dream possible. And to all educators: May this book serve as a source of inspiration and support as you continue the important work of ensuring every student succeeds.

—Josh

To my incredible children, who continue to teach me what it means to be focused on creating cultures where everyone feels lifted up and possible. To all students everywhere and their teachers: May the ideas in this book inspire hope and possibility in creating spaces and practices where all learn at high levels and develop the confidence that launches them into a life of their design.

—Nicole

Acknowledgments

I am deeply grateful to Josh and Nicole for their expertise and partnership throughout this project. Josh, you have been an incredible leader and collaborator, and I am so proud of all we have accomplished together. Nicole, thank you for taking a chance on two strangers and becoming such an integral part of this project; it truly would not be complete without you. A heartfelt thank-you as well to the board, administrators, instructional coaches, staff, and students of the Neosho School District in Neosho, Missouri. I hope this book encourages and inspires you, just as you have inspired us. Without your work, this book would not have been possible. Thank you, Solution Tree, for providing a platform dedicated to developing teacher capacity and inspiring educators to do what's best for students. It's an honor to be part of something bigger than myself.

—Autumn

I am deeply grateful to Nicole for embracing this idea from the start and for walking alongside us with steady support every step of the way. To Autumn, thank you for being such an unbelievable collaborator; I could not have asked for a better teammate in this process. I would like to thank Solution Tree for believing in this project and providing the platform to bring these ideas to life.

A special thank-you goes to my parents, John and Jamie, who have always been my biggest fans and have shaped who I am and the work I do. Finally, to my wife, Jen, and our children, Quinlyn, Cohen, and Nash, thank you for your love, patience, and encouragement. You are my greatest source of inspiration.

—Josh

I am so grateful to be in partnership with Josh and Autumn. This project was inspiring, and I learned so much as I listened to their ideas and we talked through how to create a resource that would help educators everywhere see that creating systems and practices that work for all students is not only possible, it is also absolutely essential. Thank you, Josh and Autumn, for inviting me to be part of sharing your incredible ideas and impact. I also want to shout out my parents, Tom and Judy Dimich, who support me unconditionally.

Special thanks to Solution Tree for the incredible support and guidance through the whole process. Todd, Madonna, and Laurel—your support in crafting and refining our ideas was amazing. Shavantay and Mary—I'm so grateful for all your support in marketing our resource and helping us shape the message and need. There are so many others who have lifted our work up; we are so grateful.

—Nicole

Solution Tree Press would like to thank the following reviewers:

Annika Barton
Assistant Director of Early Childhood Education
Douglas County School District
Castle Rock, Colorado

Molly Capps
Director for Student Support Services
Moore County Schools
Carthage, North Carolina

Kelli Fuller
Assistant Principal
Howard Perrin Elementary School
Benton, Arkansas

Anthony S. Golding
Principal
Pierce Street Elementary School
Tupelo, Mississippi

Alexi Cuevas Herrera
Instructional Specialist
Spradling Elementary School
Fort Smith, Arkansas

Jennifer Rasmussen
Literacy Specialist and Instructional Services Director
Cooperative Educational Service Agency No. 4
West Salem, Wisconsin

Christie C. Shealy
Director of Student Services
Anderson School District One
Williamston, South Carolina

Hope Shields
Instructional Specialist of ESL and World Languages
Moore County Schools
Carthage, North Carolina

Dawn Vang
Principal
Pembroke Elementary School
Virginia Beach, Virginia

Table of Contents

Reproducibles are in italics.

Visit **go.SolutionTree.com/RTIatWork** to download the free reproducibles in this book.

About the Authors

Autumn Mosby has served as a teacher, elementary instructional coach, and districtwide lead instructional coach for the past fifteen years at the Neosho School District in Neosho, Missouri. She is passionate about literacy, effective instructional practice and intervention, and coaching.

Autumn has worked with multiple schools in her district on creating systematic approaches to instruction and intervention practices. She partners with classroom teachers, using coaching cycles to strengthen Tier 1 and Tier 2 instruction. She also works with staff who provide Tier 3 intervention to help bridge their intervention practices with the classroom. Her work in building systems for diagnostic assessment, student progress monitoring, and targeted interventions has led to significant growth and achievement in her schools. Because of these systems, Autumn was able to help lead two schools in her district to receive Model PLC (Professional Learning Community) at Work® status, as well as level 2 High Reliability Schools certification. She has led multiple professional development sessions at both state and national levels, focusing on student-centered instruction and how the brain learns, and has published multiple articles on effective instruction and instructional theory on Edutopia.com.

Autumn has a bachelor's degree in elementary education and a master's degree in reading from Missouri State University. She is certified as a literacy coach through the University of Arkansas at Little Rock and serves as a literacy certified Solution Tree associate.

Joshua Depoe, EdD, is the executive director of academics for the Neosho School District in Neosho, Missouri. In this role, he supports curriculum, instruction, and intervention systems to ensure high levels of learning for all students. With nearly twenty years of experience in education, Joshua is known for his leadership in developing collaborative cultures, strengthening Tier 2 supports, and guiding schools through continuous improvement. Joshua is a member of the National Association of Elementary School Principals and has been recognized for his impact on instructional leadership.

Joshua had the privilege of leading Benton Elementary in the Neosho school district to earn Model PLC at Work School recognition from Solution Tree, a distinction that reflects a deep commitment to collaborative teams, a guaranteed and viable curriculum, and a relentless focus on student learning. Under his leadership, the school built strong professional learning communities, ensuring that every team regularly analyzed data, responded to student needs, and refined instruction through collective responsibility. In addition, the school earned High Reliability School level 1 and level 2 certification through Marzano Resources, demonstrating highly reliable systems for safe, supportive, and collaborative teaching and learning environments. These recognitions represent a sustained, team-driven effort to build systems that ensure high levels of learning for all students.

Joshua has a bachelor of science in education from Missouri Southern State University, a master of science in educational administration from Southwest Baptist University, an educational specialist degree from William Woods University, and a doctor of education from William Woods University.

He serves as a Beyond Labels Solution Tree associate.

Nicole Dimich has a passion for education and lifelong learning, which has led to her extensively exploring, facilitating, and implementing innovative practices in school transformation. She works with elementary and secondary educators in presentations, trainings, and consultations that address today's most critical issues, all in the spirit of facilitating increased student learning and confidence.

Nicole was a school transformation specialist, where she coached individual teachers and teams of teachers in assessment, literacy, and high expectations for all students. She was also a program evaluator and trainer at the Princeton Center for Leadership Training in Princeton, New Jersey. A former middle and high school English teacher, Nicole is committed to making schools places where all students feel invested and successful.

As one of the architects of Solution Tree's Assessment Collaborative and a featured presenter at conferences internationally, Nicole empowers educators to build their capacity for developing and implementing engaging assessment design, formative assessment practices, common assessment design and analysis, response to intervention (RTI) systems, data-driven decisions, student work protocols, and motivational strategies.

Nicole was the executive director of Thrive Ed, a nonprofit working to fundamentally transform education by empowering students, teachers, and guiding coalitions to innovate and thrive. Nicole is the author of *Design in Five: Essential Phases to Create Engaging Assessment Practice* and the coauthor of *The Handbook for Design in Five: Assessment Tools and Protocols for Teachers and Teams*. She is a coauthor of *Taking Action: A Handbook for RTI at Work, Second Edition* with colleagues Austin Buffum, Mike Mattos, Janet Malone, Luis Cruz, and Sarah Schuhl. She has coauthored multiple other books, including *Jackpot!*, *Concise Answers to Frequently Asked Questions About Assessment and Grading*, *Motivating Students*, *Growing Tomorrow's Citizens in Today's Classrooms*, *Instructional Agility*, and *Essential Assessment*. She has also contributed to the best-selling book *The Teacher as Assessment Leader* and *The Principal as Assessment Leader*.

Nicole earned a bachelor of arts degree in English and psychology from Concordia College and a master of arts degree in human development from Saint Mary's University.

To learn more about Nicole's work, visit http://allthingsassessment.info or follow her on LinkedIn or @NicoleDimich on X.

To book Autumn Mosby, Joshua Depoe, or Nicole Dimich for professional development, contact pd@SolutionTree.com.

Foreword

By Mike Mattos

It is undeniable that effective initial instruction alone will not meet the learning needs of every student. While first best teaching is the foundation of a multi-tiered system of support, ensuring all students learn at high levels requires educators to provide students interventions when Tier 1 instruction was insufficient—what the authors of this outstanding book refer to as "second helpings." Equally important, this extra help must be highly effective at targeting the specific learning needs of each student requiring additional assistance. Providing ineffective interventions wastes resources, frustrates educators, and perpetuates student failure.

While educators want effective student supports, my experience is that many schools' interventions are driven by good intentions but unfortunately misguided in their actual implementation. When I ask teachers and administrators to describe their current site interventions, the most common responses focus on three Ps: places, people and programs.

- **Places:** Many schools refer to interventions as locations. This mindset is captured in the common refrain, "Where do I send this student for help?" For example, students receiving special education support are sent to the resource room. Students demonstrating misbehaviors are sent to the office. Because interventions are provided at school, there will be an obvious need to determine where on campus each intervention will take place. But the location alone is not the intervention. And frequently these locations end up with groups of students who have broadly similar labels—they have qualified for special education services, say—but with markedly different needs. This makes targeting interventions extremely difficult.

- **People:** Similar to places, some schools refer to interventions as specific people. This approach is conveyed in the question, "Who do I send this student to?" This sends classroom teachers a message—interventions are someone else's responsibility. This mindset chips away at a collaborative approach to additional support, and it quietly builds the assumption that RTI or MTSS implementation requires hiring supplemental interventionist staff.
- **Programs:** I frequently receive questions from educators asking, "What intervention program do you recommend for Tier 3 reading support?" Or "What do you think of this particular online intervention program for mathematics?" Wouldn't it be incredible if there was a program you could buy that could make every student a confident reader, or a website where struggling mathematics students could make up all their gaps? If such programs existed, my advice would be this—If there is a program that can ensure every student learns how to read, use it at Tier 1 for initial teaching, and there will never be a need for additional reading support. Unfortunately, no such programs currently exist.

I'm not saying places, people, and programs shouldn't be part of planning additional time and support—they should. My concern is that they're supporting considerations, not the driving elements of a highly effective systemic intervention process. To prove the point, between 2020 and 2024, schools across the United States received a record 190 billion dollars of supplemental federal funding to provide interventions for students who were negatively impacted by the pandemic. Most schools and districts spent these funds on hiring additional interventionist staff, buying intervention programs, and determining where on campus to house this additional help. Yet according to the National Assessment of Educational Progress (NAEP), little progress was made toward closing achievement gaps, especially for students living in poverty (The Nation's Report Card, n.d.). While many factors may have contributed to this outcome, it is clear that hiring additional staff and buying programs did not make a significant impact.

So instead of defining interventions by places, people, and programs, I would suggest educators focus on a different set of powerful, proven Ps: processes, pedagogy, and precision.

- **Processes:** Ensuring that all students learn at high levels requires an entire school staff to work collaboratively and take collective responsibility for student learning. This means effective interventions begin by reorganizing the school and district so educators have the job-embedded time to focus their collective efforts on critical topics, including the following.

    1. Getting extremely clear on exactly what all students must learn—unit by unit—to be prepared for future success
    2. Determining how educators will frequently assess student progress on each essential standard
    3. Scheduling dedicated time for educators to collectively plan and respond when students need additional time and support to master essential curriculum
    4. Designing meaningful extensions for students who have mastered essential curriculum and are prepared to further their learning

    The best way to achieve these foundational, collaborative outcomes is for a school to fully commit to the Professional Learning Community (PLC) at Work process.

- **Pedagogy:** If an effective intervention is not a person or a program, what is it? It is good teaching! More precisely, an effective intervention is good teaching, made precise by assessment, and best delivered through collective processes.

    During Tier 1, the goal of best first teaching is for teachers to use instructional practices that are proven to meet the learning needs of most students. As teaching is both a science and an art (Marzano, 2017), allowing individual teachers some autonomy to be creative and to leverage their individual strengths is encouraged. A vast majority of educators teach the best they know every day.

    So when it comes to giving students "second helpings" of good teaching, it would be naïve to think that teachers working in isolation will individually identify better ways to reteach each essential standard. But when schools and districts function as a PLC, they have the collaborative time and focus for educators to collectively discuss and determine better ways to reteach. The power of collective efficacy is superior to the individual efficacy of teachers working alone (Hattie, 2023).

- **Precision:** If we were medical professionals, and we wanted those we served to be physically healthy, we would start by advocating for all our patients to follow the proven lifestyle habits of proper nutrition, regular exercise, and sufficient rest. These first best health practices will keep most of our patients healthy most of the time. But to ensure each individual person is healthy, we would regularly collect information to monitor the health of each person. That data lets us pinpoint each patient's strengths and needs, then build a treatment plan to match.

  As educators, we should take the same approach. The biggest difference between best first teaching (Tier 1) and the reteaching of essential standards (Tier 2) is how teacher teams use targeted assessment information on the "academic health" of each student. When done well, this creates a timely, never-ending process in which educators have dedicated collaborative time and targeted assessment data to determine the following.

  - What did each student do well? It is almost always best to build on student strengths.
  - On which essential standard—or exactly what parts of the standard—does each struggling student need additional support?
  - What was the cause of a student's errors?
  - Which of our instructional practices proved to be most effective, and which ones did not?
  - Do any of our research-based intervention programs target some of these specific learning needs?
  - Based on all the above information, what will be the best ways to reteach to meet each student's needs?
  - Since educators take collective responsibility for student learning, who would be the best staff member to provide each targeted reteaching?
  - Where will we provide each of the interventions when we collectively respond?

> Interventions work best when—with precision—students who have the exact same need are grouped together and the instructional practices being used represent the collective knowledge and skills of teachers working collaboratively.

Notice that in an effective intervention process, there is a need to consider places, people, and programs, but this comes at the end of the process and is related more to the logistics of providing additional time and support. Processes, pedagogy, and precision drive the process. Adding additional intervention staff and intervention programs to an archaic school design characterized by teachers working in isolation is akin to trying to save the *Titanic* from sinking by adding additional service staff and deck chairs.

The throughline in the collaborative processes that I have described is the use of formative assessment, especially when leveraged by teacher teams. Assessment, when done well, is one of the most powerful instructional practices educators have to improve student academic achievement and mindset (Andrade & Cizek, 2019; Brookhart et al., 2013, 2019; Goddard, Hoy, & Hoy, 2000; Goodwin & Marzano, 2022; Hattie 2023; Marzano, 2018; Skaalvik & Skaalvik, 2007). The authors of this exceptional resource have masterfully connected the power of collaboration (PLC), systematic interventions (MTSS), and assessment to guide the process. As expert practitioners, their recommendations are based on powerful research, honed by decades of working on the front lines of education, and will work regardless of the age and demographics of your students. Equally important, implementing these ideas will not require governmental approval, additional staff, buying new programs, or extending your school day.

When you read this book and put these powerful ideas into practice at your school and district, not only will you improve student learning but you will get an added bonus: It will provide much-needed support to educators, too! Research confirms that teacher retention increases when they feel part of a team and see their collective efforts make a difference for their students (Mansell & Kirksey, 2025). The PLC at Work process, when done well, is job-embedded staff development to support their learning. For in the end, everyone could use second helpings from time to time.

Introduction

Picture this: You're at home, surrounded by people you love, savoring a delicious meal. There's laughter, warmth, and an incredible aroma emanating from the kitchen. That first bite? Pure satisfaction. You finish your plate, thinking you're done—but then you return for a second helping! Not because you have to, but because the food was too good to pass up.

That moment around the dinner table? It's a fitting picture of what good teaching looks like. In schools, Tier 1 instruction, or core grade-level or course-level instruction, is like a carefully prepared first serving, designed to work for everyone. And, just like at dinner, everyone's appetite is different; some students will need more to really thrive, which we liken to Tier 2 instruction. That second helping provides just what each person needs to feel fully satisfied. At the heart of Tier 2 systems is a focus on additional time and support to ensure all students grow and achieve *at grade level or better.*

Within the RTI (response to intervention) at Work™ framework, sometimes called a multitiered system of supports (MTSS), Tier 2 instruction serves a very specific and essential purpose. Some systems may differentiate between RTI and MTSS, with RTI being a component of MTSS and MTSS being the entire school improvement framework. We align with the RTI at Work model, which uses RTI and MTSS interchangeably. The RTI at Work framework connects the work so all teams and processes play a targeted role in ensuring all students learn at high levels. RTI is designed to provide targeted, skill-specific interventions to students who are not yet proficient in essential standards, even after receiving strong Tier 1 instruction. This support is not a replacement for core instruction but a supplement to it. Students receiving Tier 2 intervention continue to participate fully in

Tier 1 learning experiences while receiving additional support on grade-level essential standards focused on their specific areas of need.

Typically delivered in smaller groups, Tier 2 instruction is data driven, timely, and focused. It is meant to be responsive and short term, with the goal of closing learning disparities quickly and getting students back on track. Teacher teams, which may be grade-level specific, course specific, vertical, or interdisciplinary, intentionally and collaboratively plan and implement interventions. They closely monitor progress to ensure students are making gains in the essential standards the team identified in their Tier 1 foundational work. From this perspective, RTI at Work and Professional Learning Communities (PLCs) at Work® are one and the same. Schools and systems become PLCs as they focus on becoming a collaborative, learning-focused, results-based culture, and teacher teams focus on addressing the four critical questions of a PLC (DuFour et al., 2024).

1. What knowledge, skills, and dispositions should every student acquire in this unit, this course, or this grade level?
2. How will we know when each student has acquired the essential knowledge and skills?
3. How will we respond when some students do not learn?
4. How will we extend the learning for students who are already proficient?

These four questions are not only the foundation of Tier 1 core instruction; they are also critical to a strong Tier 2 system. If teams don't have clarity on core instruction and what proficiency looks like (Tier 1), Tier 2 systems are ineffective and unmanageable. When schools are clear on Tier 1 instruction, they embrace the process of implementing a PLC culture and an RTI at Work system to accelerate and extend student learning in a feasible way.

In the second edition of *Taking Action: A Handbook for RTI at Work*, Mike Mattos and colleagues (2025) articulate the RTI at Work approach, which includes three key collaborative structures at the school level.

1. A guiding coalition that leads the work and maintains focus on priorities
2. Teacher teams that identify and clarify grade-level essential standards, analyze data, and respond to student learning
3. An intervention team that coordinates and ensures systematic support for students who need additional time and help on foundational skills

Together, these structures emphasize collective responsibility and a proactive, timely response to ensure learning for every student. Figure I.1 shows the RTI at Work pyramid (Mattos et al., 2025), which illustrates all three tiers of instruction in relationship to each other. The pyramid is split to clarify which team takes responsibility for each part of the system represented by the pyramid. *Second Helpings* presumes a basic level of knowledge of RTI; any readers who do not feel they have that knowledge or want to refresh should refer to *Taking Action* (Mattos et al., 2025).

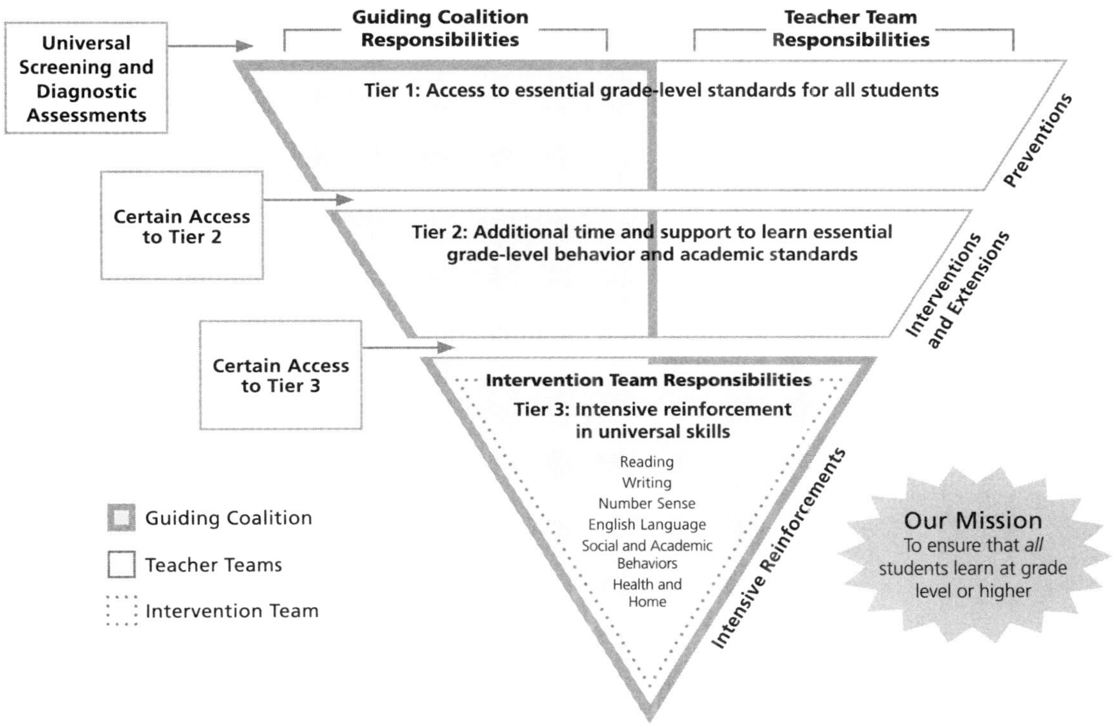

Source: Mattos et al., 2025, p. 12.

Figure I.1: The RTI at Work pyramid.

Let's take a closer look at the pivotal roles the three teams have in the successful implementation of this process.

- The **guiding coalition**, or a more specialized school leadership team that reflects many roles in the school community, leads the design and implementation of the entire RTI at Work system, including designing a master schedule and protecting time to implement the process effectively. Team members ensure students get access to grade-level essential standards in the structure of the school and teams. The guiding coalition is responsible for ensuring a structure for Tier 2 intervention time is in place. It also monitors the results of Tier 2 interventions schoolwide, adjusting and guiding reflection to ensure the system is doing what it intended: providing students the time and instruction needed to learn grade-level essentials and beyond.

- The **teacher team** determines grade-level or course-specific essential standards and maps all standards across units or time frames. Team members choose or design end-of-unit and common formative assessments to understand the impact of Tier 1 and Tier 2 instruction, which enables them to identify students who need additional time and support to learn the essential standards. These actions are foundational at Tier 1 and create the basis of a strong Tier 2 system. The teacher team takes the lead on both Tier 1 and Tier 2 instruction and intervention. At Tier 2, teacher teams collaboratively analyze common assessment evidence to determine which students need additional support on grade-level, course-specific essential standards. Teams double down on these essential standards to accelerate learning. Students with larger disparities in their foundational skills receive Tier 3 support. Some students will need both Tier 2 intervention (grade-level standards) and Tier 3 acceleration (foundational skills).
- The **intervention team** takes the lead in supporting students who need Tier 3 support in the foundational skills listed in the bottom section of the pyramid in figure I.1 (page 3). These foundational skills include reading, writing, number sense, English language, social and academic behaviors, and health and home (Mattos et al., 2025). Some students need the support of all three tiers. The intervention team, often made up of counselors, interventionists, special services, and others with expertise and roles in supporting students, creates a process for teacher teams to identify and refer students when they need more than Tier 1 instruction and Tier 2 intervention to achieve grade-level essentials. When this is working well, it reduces overidentification of students for special education.

These three teams function interdependently. Each needs to have a clear understanding of their roles and actions within the system. When the teams are successful, this leads to acceleration and closing opportunity gaps and disparities in learning (Mattos et al., 2025).

Second Helpings focuses on the practices and logistics that make Tier 2 effective. Tier 2 is not just "more of the same." It's not reteaching with the same method that didn't work the first time, and it's not a remedial program. It's also not an optional or loosely structured effort that varies from classroom to classroom—it must be systematic, intentional, and consistent across the school. Tier 2 is not and will never be a substitute for quality Tier 1 instruction, nor is it a stand-in for behavior support or a step toward special education. Rather, it's a general education responsibility, grounded in the belief that all students can learn at high levels with the right support. When implemented well, Tier 2 becomes a safety net that's proactive, precise, and built into the school day, not something students have to qualify for or chase outside of regular instruction. Additionally, Tier 2 does not focus on remediation of foundational skills, as that is the focus of Tier 3 instruction. Tier 3 is highly effective only when students have daily access to Tier 1 and Tier 2 instruction. It is an *and* not an *or* situation.

Administrators, guiding coalitions, teacher teams, interventionists, and district leaders (special services, curriculum, assessment, and so on) all need to clearly understand an effective Tier 2 system and how their role supports it. *Second Helpings* provides practical action steps for all educators with specific guidance on how to implement these systems. We have structured this book so that each chapter serves as an action step, building on the one before it. At the same time, each chapter can stand alone, validating current practices or providing guidance to address challenges you may encounter as you develop your Tier 2 system. You'll also find reproducible tools throughout the chapters, concluding with reflection questions intentionally designed for collaborative use with your team—particularly your guiding coalition. These questions are meant to spark dialogue, clarify next steps, and strengthen collective ownership of the work. Rather than serving solely as individual reflection prompts, these questions support shared decision making, alignment, and continuous improvement at the leadership level.

Chapter 1 dives into assessment, the appetizer that sets the stage for the whole learning experience. Before the main course, a good appetizer gives you a taste of what's coming and helps you figure out what you're hungry for. That's precisely what assessment does in the classroom. Assessment defines grade-level proficiency. The items and tasks teacher teams use are a check of how students respond to instruction—what's clicking, what's confusing, and who might need something extra. When done right, assessments are simple but powerful information that help teams understand what students know and still need to work on. This chapter explores the foundational work that teacher teams do at Tier 1 to set up a strong

Tier 2 system with informative assessments that give accurate insight so teachers can make thoughtful choices about who's ready to move forward and who might need another round of support to feel confident and capable.

Chapter 2 is all about planning that second course, after the Tier 1 main course. Once you've gathered the assessment results, it's time to figure out what to do with the data. That's where the team's commitment begins. When guests go for a second helping, it's thoughtful, not random. They will gravitate toward the food they can't get enough of. The hosts are willing to accommodate each guest's needs. In the same way, teams commit to identifying and ensuring students get targeted additional instruction. This chapter explains how to use simple data protocols to really dig into what the results are telling you. You'll learn how to come together as a team, make sense of the data, and build a clear, doable plan targeted to student needs that actually works. You never want to take a wild guess; rather, your team wants to be intentional and focused, ensuring every decision is supported by what your students need most.

In chapter 3, we get practical about the recipe for Tier 2 instructional design. Guests who loved the meal will often ask for the recipe for the dish they couldn't get enough of. Similarly, a teacher team creates a collective response for students who need the steps to succeed in a specific essential standard. Whether helping students who need to grasp the basics or be pushed to extend, this chapter gives the instructional recipe to make those second helpings count. You'll find scaffolding strategies, flexible groupings, and ways to differentiate without becoming overwhelmed or watering down expectations. Instructional approaches are grounded in research but delivered in a way that makes sense in real classrooms with real constraints.

But teaching isn't just about what we do. It's about how students respond. That's why chapter 4 focuses on getting students invested in their learning. Hosts identify who is coming to the dinner party and consider the needs of each guest. They will reach out and communicate the details of the meal. For Tier 2 to work, students need to understand where they stand, where they're heading, and how to bridge that gap. When students understand the *why* behind the extra support and see it as a vote of confidence rather than a red flag, they begin to believe and experience a shift in mindset. When learners become clearer about the goal and believe they can learn it, achievement follows. Learners need to see Tier 2 intervention as an opportunity, not a punishment. This chapter offers strategies for building student ownership, developing learners' belief that they can improve through effort and learning, and involving learners in their own progress.

Chapter 5 goes deeper than just content. Real learning sticks when students develop self-regulation, perseverance (sometimes referred to as *grit*), and a growth mindset. When we think about grit, we must remember that we rarely see the whole story. For some students facing trauma, bullying, or difficult home lives, simply showing up to school each day is an act of perseverance. These are not extras; rather, they are the *secret sauce* that makes learning last. In fact, the guiding coalition takes the lead on defining these characteristics at Tier 1 and ensuring that students get instruction and then additional support for learning dispositions such as self-reflection and metacognition, organization, and perseverance at Tier 2 when needed. This chapter explores how to build those essential learning dispositions that help students face challenges, bounce back from failure, and take charge of their education. In the same way that a shared meal is more than just calories, real learning is more than just standards. Real learning is building habits of mind that fuel a lifetime of growth.

Chapter 6 emphasizes that the school's master schedule directly reflects its commitment to equity and the promise to spend the time needed for each and every student to learn. We liken this to a chef understanding the time it takes to cook the meal. Tier 2 and Tier 3 supports must be intentionally built into the daily schedule, not added as afterthoughts. The chapter outlines how schools at all levels can design schedules that protect time for all three tiers of instruction.

Chapter 7 tackles the tough stuff: packed schedules, staff shortages, and limited resources. But it doesn't just name problems; it offers practical solutions and encourages schools to get creative. Whether it's flexible scheduling, reimagining how we use support staff, or embedding intervention into the school day, this chapter equips you with doable ideas to make Tier 2 sustainable and successful.

No matter what kind of event you are hosting, there will inevitably be things that don't go as planned. Flexibility is key when accommodating the needs of our guests. Sometimes it isn't as comfortable for the host, but they bend over backward for the guests. Similarly, Tier 2 systems focus on what's best for the learners and not always easiest for the adults. To be clear, "not always easiest" doesn't mean the harder route that leads to more work but rather an effective system where adult actions are doable and get results.

One message stands out throughout this book: Tier 2 isn't optional; it's essential. When done right, it's not a burden. It's our way of saying to students, "We believe in you, and we're committed to relentlessly pursing and ensuring your achievement." Think of this book as your practical guide to planning those second helpings. It's packed with tools you can use tomorrow, real examples from real classrooms, and a mindset that says we're all in this together. Just like a good host ensures nobody leaves hungry, great teachers and teacher teams ensure every student gets what they need—they're not rushed through, not overlooked, but rather supported and set up to succeed.

In the end, this work is about more than instruction. It's about belief, and it's about holding firm to the idea that every student deserves a full plate that leaves them feeling full, confident, and ready to take on whatever's next. When we feed our students well, academically, emotionally, and strategically, they grow.

So grab a seat at the dinner table. Let's talk about making Tier 2 instruction really work. When we assess thoughtfully and plan carefully, every student gets what they need—and maybe a little extra for good measure.

CHAPTER 1

Assessing to Guarantee Learning for *All*

A successful meal is often one that a good host has planned in advance with attention to detail. The first element typically involves planning the menu. A host will make decisions about what they want the meal to be, how they might decorate the table, and where to seat everyone. They will also consider their guests' preferences and dietary needs. This preplanning lays the foundation for a beautiful meal in both taste and feel. Similarly, the assessment process begins in the planning stage as teacher teams determine the evidence that will signal proficiency and identify students who need Tier 2 intervention. This is the foundational work that occurs in Tier 1: Identify essential standards and design assessments that align with them.

Gathering around a table for a meal often sparks lively conversation on a wide range of topics. Guests might comment on the enticing aroma of the food—or, if something seems off, offer a subtle remark, like, "Is something burning?" As the meal begins, everyone is quietly or openly assessing their experience: Do they enjoy the taste? The texture? Will they savor every bite or rush through? Will they go back for seconds, or are they done?

These judgments, spoken or unspoken, are all based on evidence: the flavors, texture, smell, and even the physical and social atmosphere at the table. Are the chairs comfortably spaced, or is it hard to move around? Are the interactions warm and respectful, or is there tension in the air? The dynamics among the people at the table matter too. Is there a sense of trust? Do individuals feel free to be themselves without fear of judgment? Do the people around the table notice and value each other's contributions? Do they show genuine curiosity about each other's thoughts and experiences?

Just as hosts monitor their guests' reactions to a meal, teachers monitor, assess, and intervene daily. When teacher teams come together, they gather evidence on students' status in achieving the *essential* rather than all standards. They also commit to responding to that evidence in Tier 1 (usually informed by a common formative assessment) and then again in Tier 2 (usually informed by the results of an end-of-unit assessment).

Assessment, much like a meal, requires planning before the unit begins, checking in throughout to make adjustments and assessing the final outcome. In fact, the planning and preparation for the meal often takes more time than the meal itself. If a host rushes through the prep and planning, the meal can easily be chaotic and disjointed. This is true for a teacher team too. If a teacher team doesn't spend the time in the preplanning, specifically designing a grade-level end-of-unit assessment, the Tier 2 intervention can feel unattainable and ineffective.

Assessment, both in preparation and throughout instruction, is central to the teacher team's understanding of which students have mastered the essential standards and which students need additional time and support through Tier 2 intervention. Many of the assessment actions that make Tier 2 effective depend on the actions teams took at Tier 1. If Tier 1 work is not solid, Tier 2 may feel overwhelming.

In this chapter, we outline the assessment practices that make Tier 2 intervention manageable, targeted, and effective. We also identify the critical role of essential standards and the unpacking of those standards to find learning goals, or targets, to craft learning progressions and scoring agreements that define proficiency or mastery. Finally, we describe the importance of developing a unit assessment plan to ensure an accurate end-of-unit assessment that aligns with the rigor of the standard at grade level and ensures a thoughtful instructional design.

The Purpose of Assessment

Assessment, or evidence of learning, plays a central role in guiding teacher teams to identify which students need Tier 2 intervention on which essential standards. At its best, assessment evidence clearly describes when a student has met proficiency or mastery on a grade-level standard. This assessment evidence helps teams of teachers do three things: (1) evaluate the impact of initial instruction, (2) determine which students need a reteach, different instruction, or intervention to achieve the essential standards, and (3) develop and plan the Tier 2 intervention for the identified students based on the misconceptions found in the assessment evidence. When used as a source of actionable information, assessment becomes the driving force behind a successful and impactful RTI at Work system, ensuring student achievement, student confidence, and teacher efficacy. However, it is important to understand which types of assessments best inform Tier 2 interventions and which do not.

Large-scale assessments, such as state or provincial exams, the SAT, ACT, or Advanced Placement tests, are designed to provide data on system performance over time. These assessments are best used to analyze trends and understand how groups of students respond to the educational system. While these measures are important for accountability and broad curriculum decisions, they are not designed to inform day-to-day teaching or identify specific learning needs of individual students (Allensworth, Correa, & Ponisciak, 2008; Brookhart, McTighe, Stiggins, & Wiliam, 2019; Levitan & Munyan-Penney, 2024a; Munyan-Penney & Mehrotra, 2023). Because this data reveals which groups of students are not being served well overall, guiding coalitions and district-level teams can use this information to understand the impact of systems and curriculum and instruction approaches over time. But the key to changing the results is focusing on the actionable assessment data at the classroom level from end-of-unit assessments and common formative assessments that directly align to grade-level standards.

The same is true for benchmark assessments, which are typically given two to three times a year. Benchmark assessments help students experience the standardized test method and reflect on how to best take tests in these contexts. Teachers can provide test-taking strategies for these contexts as well. If benchmark assessments align to the standards that teams intended students to learn, the data may help inform Tier 2 intervention and the effectiveness of instruction to date. But if the benchmark assessments assess standards not yet taught, students don't need intervention as they haven't yet been exposed to those standards or expected to learn them.

Importantly, large-scale assessments are not the championship game of learning. Such all-or-nothing frames add stress for students and teacher teams, shifting their energy from ensuring essential standard learning to test preparation, which does not help students take the test more seriously (Almarzouki, 2024; Barbayannis et al., 2022; Gobena, 2024; Ng, Koh, & Chia, 2003). These assessments are a snapshot—a data point for educators to understand how the system is functioning. Extensive practice with those formats does not guarantee success. Rather, it leads to test fatigue for both students and educators.

In contrast, classroom-level assessments, such as end-of-unit assessments and common formative assessments, are far more actionable for teachers. These assessments directly align to the standards and learning targets (or all the parts of learning that lead to achieving the whole standard) students are expected to master. As such, these assessments provide the most valuable insight into what students need next in their learning journeys. When designed well, these assessments serve as the foundation for effective Tier 2 interventions, indicating which students need more time on grade-level standards.

When students master essential standards, develop key cognitive and self-regulation skills, and build confidence, they demonstrate achievement at a higher level (Allensworth et al., 2008; Brookhart & McMillan, 2020; Wiliam & Leahy, 2024). Fostering student investment (see chapter 4) and cultivating learning dispositions (see chapter 5) are major actions in Tier 2 intervention systems because of their incredible impact on student results (Andrade & Brookhart, 2020; Andrade & Cizek, 2010; Brookhart & McMillan, 2020). When students approach an assessment with more confidence, they will persist when it gets tough, which leads to better scores.

Teacher teams must design classroom assessments to accurately measure *essential standards* or the *intended learning*, not just mimic the format of large-scale tests. Overemphasizing test preparation or mirroring all classroom tasks to standardized formats can be counterproductive. This approach can lead to assessment fatigue, reduce student engagement, narrow curriculum, and diminish the formative power of classroom assessment (Allensworth et al., 2008; Brookhart et al., 2019; Dysarz, 2018b; Levitan & Munyan-Penney, 2024a; Munyan-Penney & Mehrotra, 2023). Students may begin to see assessments as merely a means to a score rather than a tool to support growth and reflection that lead to essential learning.

To ensure students reach grade-level proficiency or mastery of the essential standards, teacher teams design assessments at grade level no matter where their students are in achievement. Teams must commit to analyzing end-of-unit common assessment evidence to determine what specific skills students need to develop. This work is most effective when grounded in a clear learning progression and straightforward definitions of what proficiency looks like (such as in the form of scoring agreements), as well as when teacher teams agree on what to prioritize. When teachers align instruction with the most essential learning and provide practice time, students can improve both their skills and confidence.

Research supports this. When students receive access to grade-level content and assessments, and when those are coupled with meaningful instructional responses, they achieve at higher levels (Brookhart & McMillan, 2020; Dysarz, 2018b; Levitan & Munyan-Penney, 2024a; Munyan-Penney & Mehrotra, 2023; Wiliam & Leahy, 2024). Meeting students where they are is rooted in care, but if educators over-scaffold or lower expectations, they risk denying students the opportunity to work at the level that fosters deep learning. Students learn best when schools prioritize *access to grade-level content* paired with scaffolds rather than lowering expectations through remediation. Evidence from state guidance, policy analyses, and large-scale studies confirms that acceleration strategies close learning disparities more effectively and promote equity (Hamilton, Kaufman, & Diliberti, 2020; Michigan Association of Intermediate School Administrators, 2023; TNTP, 2023).

Assessment evidence is key to both effective feedback and targeted instruction that accelerate student learning. When teacher teams clarify what students know, identify what they need (based on quality grade-level assessment), and then focus on those areas with precision, learning occurs. When students receive feedback that is timely, specific, and connected to success criteria, they are better able to self-assess, adjust, and improve. Teacher teams can't respond to everything, so assessment must be accurate and aligned to the most essential standards to make feedback processes and intervention effective and doable. The next section articulates the assessment actions teams take to set up effective Tier 2 systems.

Assessment in Action

To ensure a high-quality Tier 2 intervention system and informative assessment, teacher teams engage in the following foundational actions, as Mattos and colleagues (2025) describe in *Taking Action*.

- Identifying essential standards
- Designing a unit assessment plan
- Creating assessments and beginning Tier 1 instruction
- Planning for student investment
- Developing protocols to analyze assessment evidence (both common formative assessments and end-of-unit assessments) to plan Tier 1 instruction and Tier 2 intervention

This prework is central to data analysis that leads to effective and targeted Tier 2 intervention. If Tier 1 planning and instruction are not strong and well implemented, then teacher teams will have way too many students needing Tier 2 intervention, and it will be difficult to manage. Teacher teams must first engage in foundational work at Tier 1, consisting of the five essential actions Mattos and colleagues (2025) identify. We explore those five actions in the following sections.

1. Identify Essential Standards

Teacher teams identify essential standards, also referred to as *priority standards*, for both academic and behavioral outcomes. To uphold high expectations, teacher teams begin by identifying essential standards or learning outcomes from their grade-level standards whether or not students are ready to engage in those grade-level standards. These standards are not the only ones teachers teach and assess, but they are the standards the team commits to intervening on. Paula Maeker and Jacqueline Heller (2023) describe them as *promise standards*—those standards the team promises to relentlessly help students learn. Essential standards are critical in ensuring an effective and feasible Tier 2 system. Defining proficiency, or mastery, is another part of determining essential standards so teachers agree on when students have achieved the essential standards. Teams unpack their essential standards to identify learning goals, also referred to as *learning targets*. *Learning goals* are the pieces students need to learn to achieve the whole standard. Teams also identify *success criteria*, which are the qualities students need to demonstrate in their work and assessments to achieve the learning targets and standards. These qualities help create a scoring guide to further clarify which students will need Tier 2 intervention on grade-level essential standards. If teams are new to unpacking, we recommend they consult chapter 3 of *Taking Action* (Mattos et al., 2025) or chapter 3 of *Design in Five* (Dimich, 2024) for a more detailed process.

2. Design a Unit Assessment Plan

Once teacher teams select essential standards for a unit of study, team members collaboratively choose assessment methods, or types of questions, that align to the defined essential standards or learning goals they created when they unpacked the essential standards. The unit assessment plan identifies both the common formative assessments (often used to inform Tier 1 instruction) and the end-of-unit assessments (often used to inform Tier 2 intervention). End-of-unit assessments are administered at the end of the unit or instructional period, when students are expected to demonstrate some degree of mastery. Teachers will use this assessment to determine which students need Tier 2 intervention. Teachers often use common formative assessments, which they typically administer before the end of the unit, to inform Tier 1 core instruction. Some teacher teams, however, may use common formative assessments to provide Tier 2 instruction during the unit and not just after the unit has ended. This process is commonly known as *backward design*, where teacher teams define what they want students to learn in the unit and how they will measure or assess proficiency or mastery at the end of the unit before the unit begins.

3. Create Common Assessments and Begin Instruction

After teacher teams craft their unit assessment plan, they design or select the actual assessment questions or items they identified in the assessment plan. To ensure a solid assessment, adhere to the following criteria of what assessment items should do.

- Align to a grade-level essential standard or learning goal (whether students are at grade level or not)
- Be at the appropriate cognitive level
- Ensure students perform the verb in the standard or learning goal; for example, if the verb in the standard is *explain*, students must produce an explanation rather than just select one
- Be accompanied by a plan and timeline to administer it
- Be accompanied by a plan for when teacher teams will analyze the results of the common formative assessment or end-of-unit assessment
- Be accompanied by a plan for when and how teacher teams will respond to the results for students who need additional time and instruction or intervention based on the end-of-unit assessment; this is where schools and the guiding coalition in particular ensure Tier 2 time is planned in the schedule (see chapter 6 for more on scheduling)

Assessment items or questions should reflect grade-level expectations so that assessments measure what the students need to achieve (or the grade-level standard), not where they currently are. In choosing or designing the items or questions, teams further define proficiency or mastery collaboratively for each essential standard.

Importantly, end-of-unit assessments are designed at *grade level*, as student misunderstandings or gaps in prerequisite knowledge often emerge through their errors on appropriately rigorous tasks. As such, assessing below grade level is generally unnecessary and may obscure the true source of student struggles or cause fatigue, since students don't need to answer prerequisite questions as well as ones on the level of the standard. If students make mistakes on items at the standard level, the misconceptions that appear in their work can help teacher teams understand the prerequisites they don't know. Teacher teams do not need a series of questions to understand that. Prerequisite learning targets should be handled in ongoing instruction.

Assessment design signals the expected level of proficiency. For instance, a multiple-choice assessment carries a different cognitive demand than a constructed-response assessment. The validity of the assessment hinges on how well it elicits the thinking or cognitive processes called for by the standard. If a standard asks students to analyze the impact of a character's actions on a theme, students must engage in that analysis, likely through a written explanation or a structured graphic organizer. Asking students to choose from prewritten responses, as in a multiple-choice format, significantly reduces the cognitive rigor and fails to fully assess the intended learning. Maintaining high expectations, therefore, goes beyond selecting grade-level standards; it also requires that teams reach shared agreement on what *evidence of mastery* looks like in student work or responses to assessment questions. These are important components to consider as teams choose or design items for the end-of-unit assessment. This is the data teacher teams will use to determine which students need Tier 2 intervention.

After teacher teams have designed or chosen the end-of-unit assessment, members map out instruction that will lead to students mastering the intended learning of the unit, as measured by the end-of-unit assessment. As Tier 1 instruction unfolds, teachers use common formative assessments to monitor progress and identify students who may require additional time and support. Sometimes, the common formative assessment can lead to Tier 2 intervention before the end of the unit. The most important thing is that Tier 2 is a collective response by the team. High-quality assessment data is critical for determining which students need Tier 2 intervention, what specific concepts or skills they are struggling with, and what types of instructional responses will be most effective. Creating the assessment and first instruction effectively is key to a manageable Tier 2 system.

4. Foster Student Investment

Student investment is key in ensuring both Tier 2 intervention and Tier 1 instruction focus on learning and not just completing assignments or assessments. Teachers engage in assessment and instruction practices that guide students to address three questions: Where am I going? Where am I now? and How do I close the gap? The answers to these questions emerge throughout the unit and beyond, ensuring students understand that the additional time and support are not punishment but part of a culture that believes they can and will learn. Chapter 4 describes the purpose and actions for student investment in Tier 2.

5. Analyze and Respond to Common Assessment Data

Teachers analyze the evidence from both end-of-unit and common formative assessments. This analysis is not based on overall scores but broken down by standard and learning target. This means each student has a score on the learning targets or success criteria that teacher teams determined to be a component of proficiency on essential standards. This way teams can identify which learning targets need work for each student. Sometimes, teams will analyze the student work to identify the misconceptions, thus using the data to group students by like misconceptions or need. Teams also reflect on which instructional strategies have been effective and which haven't, using that insight to guide a collective response different from their first instruction.

This process is not about evaluating individual teachers; rather, it's about learning from what's working and ensuring all students receive what they need to be successful, gain confidence, and achieve the essential standards. This stage of analysis is also an ideal time to engage specialists, such as special education and multilingual teachers. These colleagues bring valuable expertise that can inform instructional responses and guide intervention design, rooted in real-time, standards-based evidence. Chapter 2 provides data protocols and guidance on analyzing assessment evidence, and chapter 3 provides guidance on targeted instruction in Tier 2 intervention.

Essential Tier 2 Teacher Team Protocols and Tools

Effective Tier 2 intervention depends on a foundation of strong Tier 1 instruction and intentional team collaboration. There is a common tendency to refer students performing below grade level to a program or specialist, with the hope that they will catch up outside the classroom. However, meaningful support begins in the classroom with high-quality Tier 1 instruction and timely, targeted Tier 2 intervention informed by common assessments that identify student needs. Those most qualified to teach students in a particular course or grade level should deliver both Tier 1 and Tier 2 instruction on grade-level essential standards. For instance, since biology teachers are the most qualified to teach biology standards, they should teach both Tier 1 instruction and Tier 2 intervention.

The following sections further describe teacher team protocols and tools often used in Tier 1 but also essential to Tier 2 success. Scoring agreements guide how to group students for Tier 2 intervention. Assessment design accuracy ensures items assess appropriately so that the errors (or extension opportunities) that emerge from the assessment evidence align with essential standards rather than behavior or missing work. The unit assessment plan ensures an aligned approach to instructional design, reducing the number of students needing Tier 2 intervention to make the system doable and effective.

Scoring Agreements

Scoring agreements emerge from a team's process of analyzing standards, sometimes called *unpacking* or *deconstructing* standards (Kramer, Sonju, Mattos, & Buffum, 2021). Often, teams develop a learning progression or proficiency scale. If teams have started or even completed this work in the past, they reference any district or school documents that help define the essential standards and descriptions of proficiency.

When designing proficiency levels or scoring agreements, teams analyze the standards, determine learning targets, and put them in a progression indicating which learning goals are prerequisites, which are at the level of the standard, and which are extensions. This is often a familiar process. In fact, some educators may groan at the thought of unpacking standards again. Unfortunately, educators may often be isolated when they undertake that process of determining what proficiency looks like, including which student work or assessment items, questions, and tasks will indicate students' proficiency levels. The process of unpacking and then choosing assessment items or student work is where educators gain clarity on what it means for students to achieve the essential standard. Teacher teams unpack standards or learning outcomes and create a progression or a set of learning targets that represent what all students must learn to achieve the standard. As they identify on-grade-level targets, teams define the criteria for student proficiency, often called *success criteria*. These success criteria are critical in understanding which part of the standard students know and which they need to work on.

Without a clear understanding of what students are expected to learn at grade level, Tier 2 systems will struggle and cannot compensate for unclear Tier 1 preparation and instruction. In some cases, Tier 2 will fall into the trap of deciding students require Tier 2 intervention simply because they haven't finished work rather than because they must develop a skill to achieve the standard. This is sometimes because proficiency and assessment evidence are not tightly aligned with learning the essential standards.

Defining proficiency sets up targeted and effective Tier 2 intervention. Assessment is the way teams understand which students need to work on what part of the essential standard. Let's be crystal clear: Teacher teams take the lead on Tier 2 intervention, as they are the experts in teaching grade-level and course-level standards.

Figure 1.1 is an example of scoring agreements that guide and define when students have met proficiency as well as what they need to work on to achieve mastery and beyond. The scoring agreement in figure 1.1 was developed by a fourth-grade teacher team to clarify their definition of proficiency. Once team members define proficiency, they analyze common assessment data and group students based on

Essential Standard Scoring Agreements		
Essential Standard: RL.4.2—Determine a theme of a story, drama, or poem from details in the text; summarize the text.		
Proficient (Success Criteria)	**Close to Proficient**	**Far From Proficient**
• Applies the meaning of academic vocabulary • Uses context clues to identify the theme • Uses text evidence to support the theme • Summarizes the most important events	• Identifies the meaning of academic vocabulary • Identifies text evidence to support a theme • Identifies challenges the character faces • Retells the story in sequence	• Shows limited or no knowledge of academic vocabulary • Identifies few to no story elements • Identifies few to no character challenges
Essential Standard: RL.4.3—Describe in depth a character, setting, or event in a story or drama, drawing on specific details in the text.		
Proficient (Success Criteria)	**Close to Proficient**	**Far From Proficient**
• Applies the meaning of academic vocabulary • Describes a character's motivations, traits, and feelings using text evidence • Explains how the setting affects the story • Explains how important events move the story forward	• Identifies the meaning of academic vocabulary • Identifies story elements • Identifies descriptive words in the text • Identifies cause-and-effect relationships within the text	• Shows limited or no knowledge of academic vocabulary • Fails to use text to describe characters, settings, or events • Identifies few to no story elements

Source for standard: National Governors Association Center for Best Practices [NGA] & Council of Chief State School Officers [CCSSO], 2010a.

Figure 1.1: Scoring agreement for essential standards—Elementary English language arts.

Visit ***go.SolutionTree.com/RTIatWork*** *for a free reproducible version of this figure.*

the qualities for each level of achievement. Chapter 2 further articulates how to structure common assessment analysis so Tier 2 targets students' learning needs for achieving the essential standards. This includes the team scoring a small sample of assessments together to ensure accuracy and calibration across teachers. Scoring agreements are necessary to ensure effective targeting of Tier 2 intervention.

Figure 1.2 is an example of a secondary biology scoring agreement. The success criteria further articulate what mastery looks like, leading to scoring agreements on any assessment and the intervention needed to ensure learning. This biology team chose two essential standards to focus their Tier 2 intervention.

Essential Standard Scoring Agreements for High School Biology		
Essential Standard: HS-LS3-3—Apply concepts of statistics and probability to explain the variation and distribution of expressed traits in a population.		
Proficient (Success Criteria)	**Close to Proficient**	**Far From Proficient**
• Accurately interprets data on trait variation using statistical measures • Applies probability concepts (for example, Punnett squares, percentages, ratios) to predict outcomes • Communicates clearly with evidence, using visuals such as histograms or scatterplots • Explains logically how genetics and environmental factors shape population traits • Connects learning to meaningful biological contexts beyond the classroom	• Identifies some ways traits vary in a population • Uses basic statistics (mean, median, range) or simple probability to describe traits • Describes simple patterns of distribution using visuals (such as charts or graphs) • Uses data in a general way to describe variation • Gives examples and makes some connections to traits in populations	• Recognizes that individuals in a population may look different but can't explain why • Names some statistical terms but struggles to apply them • Lists or notices that traits are present • Points to data but struggles to explain it • Gives simple examples but can't explain the science
Essential Standard: CCSS.ELA-LITERACY.RST.9-10.4—Determine the meaning of symbols, key terms, and other domain-specific words and phrases as they are used in a specific scientific or technical context relevant to grades 9-10 texts and topics.		

Proficient (Success Criteria)	Close to Proficient	Far From Proficient
• Accurately determines the meaning of symbols, key terms, and domain-specific words in scientific or technical texts • Uses context clues and text features to clarify the meaning of technical vocabulary • Explains how specific terms support understanding of scientific concepts or processes • Connects vocabulary meaning to examples in scientific investigations or real-world contexts • Communicates understanding of terms clearly in writing and discussion	• Identifies some symbols or key terms but may need help explaining their meaning • Uses some context clues to guess the meaning of new terms • Describes how a few words or phrases relate to scientific ideas • Connects vocabulary to examples with some support • Uses some scientific terms in explanations but not always correctly	• Recognizes scientific words but can't explain what they mean • Has difficulty using context clues to figure out new vocabulary • Can't explain how terms connect to scientific concepts • Struggles to give examples of scientific vocabulary in context • Rarely uses scientific or technical vocabulary

Source for standard: NGA & CCSSO, 2010a; NGSS Lead States, 2013.

Figure 1.2: Scoring agreement for essential standards—High school biology.

Visit ***go.SolutionTree.com/RTIatWork*** *for a free reproducible version of this figure.*

There are many different formats teacher teams may use to define proficiency or make scoring agreements on essential standards. The following list can help teams guide the critique of their scoring agreements in whatever format they may appear.

- Do the success criteria clarify what proficiency looks like for the learning target or essential standard?
- Are the success criteria specific and observable?
- Do the success criteria align with the cognitive demand of the standard versus prerequisites?
- Can students use the success criteria to self-assess or reflect?
- Are the success criteria written in student-friendly language?
- Are we using the success criteria to guide feedback and instruction or intervention?

Assessment Design

Assessment design occurs in crafting an assessment plan to ensure team members are clear about what proficiency looks like and about what and when they will administer common formative assessments and end-of-unit assessments. Assessment design also entails creating assessment questions. The end-of-unit assessment, often called a *common assessment* or *collaborative assessment*, is the best evidence of which students need Tier 2 intervention. Teacher teams design common assessments when they teach the same course or grade level, ensuring their standards are in common. A collaborative assessment signals that a team will collectively analyze and develop a response, but the team may be vertical—for instance, a kindergarten teacher, a first-grade teacher, and a second-grade teacher, or a team of one mathematics teacher each from grades six, seven, and eight. Therefore, their assessments may be loosely aligned but not in common because they teach different grade levels. A collaborative team may also be interdisciplinary, made up of teachers teaching different courses or content areas. In this case, they agree to collaborate on assessments that measure essential standards, but they take turns analyzing assessment evidence because they aren't teaching the same thing.

Sometimes teachers use common formative assessments to provide Tier 2 instruction throughout the unit. Either way, it is critical that teacher teams choose or design items and tasks that give them accurate information. Teacher teams ensure the end-of-unit assessment aligns with the intended standards that students were to master during that timeline or unit, paying special attention to the essential standards and ensuring they are accurately measured. It is important that the end-of-unit assessment and often even the common formative assessment assess at grade level, no matter what students may or may not be ready for. This is key to high levels of learning. When analyzing data, the team will determine what type of instruction students need to get them to the grade-level standard and beyond. The assessment must be at grade level and signal the ideal and intended proficiency level.

In addition, teams may select learning targets to formatively assess and respond to before the end of the unit to reduce the need for Tier 2 intervention at the end of the unit. When choosing learning targets to commonly or collaboratively assess, the goal is for teams to collectively analyze and respond and not for an individual teacher to have to respond without their colleagues' input. The common assessment is *common* when all teachers from the same grade level or course administer it. The response is collaboratively designed and executed. The teachers on the team, whether interdisciplinary or vertical, collaboratively analyze the assessment and sometimes respond to intervention individually or collectively.

In the analysis stage, teams will review student work and the data to understand the misconceptions and determine students' next steps for learning and achieving the essential standards. Then, teams will collectively plan the instructional move (different from the initial Tier 1 instruction) to plan and design the Tier 2 intervention instructional strategy. Chapters 2 and 3 will dive deeper into how to analyze the data and match instructional interventions for Tier 2. The key factor in what assessment to analyze for Tier 2 intervention is that the assessment must be at grade level.

To ensure a targeted analysis to set up Tier 2 intervention, backward planning is essential. Figure 1.3 is a graphic organizer that represents the relationship among learning targets from essential standards, success criteria, items on the end-of-unit assessment, and common or collaborative formative assessments teams analyze to determine misconceptions, along with accompanying instruction or intervention strategies.

Teams should ensure they are clear on the learning targets and success criteria, along with the assessment evidence used to measure proficiency. Then, they intentionally analyze the assessment evidence and respond. Finally, teacher teams check in and reassess students to determine the effectiveness of their Tier 2 intervention. Figure 1.3 and figure 1.4 (page 24) are two general snapshot examples of what the foundational planning might look like. In figure 1.3, a grade 4 mathematics team chose its essential standard. The team provides descriptions of learning targets, assessment methods, potential misconceptions, and interventions. In figure 1.4, a biology team predetermines the learning targets, assessments, and misconceptions so that when they analyze student work, they are set up for Tier 2 intervention.

Unit: Fractions

Duration: Four weeks

Essential Standard: 4.NF.A.2—Compare two fractions with different numerators and different denominators, e.g., by creating common denominators or numerators, or by comparing to a benchmark fraction such as $\frac{1}{2}$. Recognize that comparisons are valid only when the two fractions refer to the same whole. Record the results of comparisons with symbols >, =, or <, and justify the conclusions, e.g., by using a visual fraction model.

Figure 1.3: Grade 4 mathematics unit assessment plan example.

continued ▶

Learning Target or Essential Standard	I can compare two fractions and explain why my answer is correct.
Success Criteria ("This means I can . . . ")	I recognize that fractions must refer to the same whole. I use >, =, or < correctly when comparing. I explain comparisons using number lines or visuals.
End-of-Unit Assessment	The assessment included multiple constructed-response items asking students to compare pairs of fractions and explain their reasoning using visuals and comparison symbols.
Common Formative Assessment	Midway through the unit, this assessment asked students to compare fractions with the same denominator and justify their answers using pictures or number lines.
Possible Misconceptions	Students may not be able to see there are different ways to express wholeness.
Instruction or Intervention	Make a few sets of visual representations of different fractions.

Source for standard: NGA & CCSSO, 2010b.

Visit ***go.SolutionTree.com/RTIatWork*** *for a free reproducible version of this figure.*

Unit: Genetics

Duration: Four weeks

Essential Standards:

CCSS.ELA-LITERACY.RST.9-10.4—Determine the meaning of symbols, key terms, and other domain-specific words and phrases as they are used in a specific scientific or technical context relevant to grades 9-10 texts and topics.

HS-LS3-3—Apply concepts of statistics and probability to explain the variation and distribution of expressed traits in a population.

Learning Target or Essential Standard	**CCSS.ELA-LITERACY.RST.9-10.4:** Determine the meaning of symbols, key terms, and other domain-specific words and phrases as they are used in a specific scientific or technical context relevant to grades 9-10 texts and topics.

Success Criteria ("This means I can . . . ")	The student accurately determines the meaning of symbols, key terms, and domain-specific words in scientific or technical texts. The student uses context clues and text features to clarify the meaning of technical vocabulary. The student explains how specific terms support understanding of scientific concepts or processes. The student connects vocabulary meaning to examples in scientific investigations or real-world contexts. The student communicates understanding of terms clearly in writing and discussion.
End-of-Unit Assessment	The assessment includes scenarios with explanations.
Common Formative Assessment	The assessment includes a scenario where students identify and describe the key terms.
Possible Misconceptions	Students may not understand the connection between genes, alleles, and traits.
Instruction or Intervention	Students revise their responses to the scenario in pairs, drawing an infographic to explain. Instructor demonstrates step-by-step Punnett square modeling.

Learning Target or Essential Standard	**HS-LS3-3:** Apply concepts of statistics and probability to explain the variation and distribution of expressed traits in a population.
Success Criteria ("This means I can . . . ")	The student accurately interprets data on trait variation using statistical measures. The student applies probability concepts (for example, Punnett squares, percentages, ratios) to predict outcomes. The student communicates clearly with evidence, using visuals like histograms or scatterplots. The student explains logically how genetics and environment shape population traits. The student connects learning to meaningful biological contexts beyond the classroom.
End-of-Unit Assessment	The assessment includes constructed responses based on a scenario. The constructed response involves creating visuals to predict outcomes and explain reasoning.

Figure 1.4: Biology unit assessment plan example.

continued ▶

Common Formative Assessment	The assessment includes sample Punnett squares and a sample scenario with constructed-response questions.
Possible Misconceptions	Students may not be able to differentiate genetic and lifestyle-based risks. Students may have difficulty building written justifications based on genetics data.
Instruction or Intervention	DNA > mRNA > protein > trait flowcharting Interactive simulation (for example, modeling mutations and traits) Family history case studies Minilessons on epigenetics and gene-environment interaction Sentence starters and claim-evidence-reasoning (CER) structure Critiquing and revising sample items

Source for standard: NGA & CCSSO, 2010a; NGSS Lead States, 2013.

Once the team has created its plan, members create the student documents or the actual common end-of-unit assessment.

The final tool and action to ensure assessment accuracy is a protocol to vet your assessment. This works well when you already have an assessment designed and want to revise it for closer alignment with the essential standard and ensure it is at grade level. The checklist guides teacher teams through questions on the clarity of the measured learning that the assessment design must set up. Questions then move into item analysis, where teachers ensure that the items are at the required and desired cognitive level. Teams often refer to different cognitive level frameworks to determine the level, such as Benjamin Bloom's (1956) taxonomy or Norman Webb's (1997) Depth of Knowledge model. The big idea is that the item requires students to perform the verb in the standard or target. Finally, questions ask teacher teams to consider how students will make sense of their results. This is one part of building student investment. Chapter 4 provides more guidance on student investment.

Figure 1.5 is a protocol adapted from *Design in Five* (Dimich, 2024) and *Taking Action* (Mattos et al., 2025) for teams to critique and revise an end-of-unit assessment, with the goal of ensuring their assessment evidence for identifying which students need Tier 2 intervention is accurate and meaningful.

Vetting Your Assessment

Use this protocol to determine the strengths and necessary revisions in your assessment. It provides questions to guide your team's review and critique of an end-of-unit assessment or common formative assessment.

1. Are the standards in the assessment clear? Is it clear what learning the assessment is measuring? (For example, does the assessment clearly state the standards or criteria?)

2. Do the learning targets represent the most important goals for this particular assessment at this particular time?

3. Do the learning targets or standards match the assessment plan, if created? If the assessment is assessing more than the essentials, is it clear which learning targets and standards are essential?

4. Are the question items or student tasks (what students produce or solve) aligned to the standard or learning target the appropriate cognitive level and on grade level (particularly if the assessment is at the end of a unit or culminating)? Use the table below to align your assessment to standards. Adjust accordingly.

Learning Target	Question Items or Tasks (what students produce or solve)	Cognitive Level (or at grade level or not)

Figure 1.5: Assessment vetting protocol.

continued ▶

5. Does the assessment represent a mix of methods, or will students have the opportunity to show their understanding in multiple ways over time (on this or other learning targets across the unit or year)?

6. Does the assessment have a clear purpose? Do teachers and students know how the assessment results will be used?

7. Do the structure, layout, and setup of questions create the best possible conditions for students to show their understanding? Does the assessment have ample white space and a clear sequence? Does it have sections that make sense and guide students through the assessment?

8. Are the directions present, clear, and concise? Does the visual layout of the assessment make it easy to understand and read?

9. If utilizing a technology tool, do students have the training needed to use the tool meaningfully? Do they have access to and an understanding of what they need to utilize the tool?

10. Are the assessment questions or exercises well written? Are they clear, succinct, and not confusing?

11. Are the assessment questions written in such a way that the answer to one question does not give away the answer to another?

12. Is there anything in the assessment itself or in the conditions in which students will take it that could produce inaccurate evidence of student learning?

13. Will students identify strengths and next steps or reflect on how the assessment impacts their learning?

Assessment Strengths:

Assessment Considerations for Revision:

Source: Adapted from Dimich, 2024; Mattos et al., 2025.

*Visit **go.SolutionTree.com/RTIatWork** for a free reproducible version of this figure.*

Accurate assessment design is essential to plan targeted Tier 2 intervention that ensures students receive instruction and intervention that will help them achieve the essential standards.

Are You Ready?

Schools and districts undertake the important prep work of beginning with the end in mind. To what extent are your school and teams prepared to engage in targeted and collaborative Tier 2 intervention? The work of identifying essential standards and matching end-of-unit assessments to those essential standards is critical in making sure Tier 2 is targeted and not just addressing general performance or students who aren't turning in work. The foundational work at Tier 1 is the basis for not being overwhelmed by needing to address too many different areas to reach grade-level standards. The system will feel like a burden if strong Tier 1 practices are not in place.

If Tier 2 is feeling like just one more thing and too much to navigate, review teacher team actions in Tier 1 and consider whether teachers have implemented those actions intentionally. If not, or if there is a new understanding of their importance, start with those actions—specifically, the first three actions (Mattos et al., 2025), reviewed here.

1. Identify essential standards, which includes unpacking these essential standards into learning targets and success criteria.
2. Design a unit assessment plan for the end-of-unit assessment and common formative assessments.
3. Create common assessments and begin instruction.

This chapter articulates that effective Tier 2 intervention begins long before teachers identify which students need additional support. Just as a successful meal depends on thoughtful planning, strong Tier 2 systems depend on teacher teams doing strong assessment work. This includes the essential Tier 1 work of identifying priority standards, unpacking them into clear learning goals and success criteria, and designing accurate grade-level assessments that reveal what students know and need next. This chapter highlights assessment as actionable evidence—not simply a score—and explains how common formative and end-of-unit assessments help teams evaluate instruction, identify misconceptions, define proficiency, and plan targeted responses. Ultimately, the chapter shows that when assessment is intentional, aligned, and collaborative, it becomes the foundation for manageable, meaningful Tier 2 intervention that builds student learning, confidence, and teacher efficacy.

After your team has assessed your readiness, use the reflection questions in the reproducible tool "Pause and Take Action: Chapter 1" to determine the next steps to build your Tier 2 intervention system.

Pause and Take Action: Chapter 1

Consider the following questions to determine your teacher team's next assessment actions.

- To what extent have we thoughtfully and intentionally executed the five essential actions in Tier 1 so that Tier 2 isn't making up for a weak Tier 1 practice?
    1. Identifying essential standards
    2. Designing a unit assessment plan
    3. Creating the actual assessments and beginning Tier 1 instruction
    4. Planning for student investment
    5. Analyzing assessment evidence (both common formative assessments and end-of-unit assessments) to plan Tier 1 instruction and Tier 2 intervention
- How are we currently designing and using success criteria from our assessment unit plans?
    - How do students engage with the success criteria during learning?
    - In what ways can we improve clarity and usefulness of success criteria?
    - Have we developed scoring agreements and processes to ensure consistency across the team when using criteria for feedback and scoring?
- What assessment evidence do we currently use to inform Tier 2 interventions? Are the questions and student tasks at grade level?
- How do we collectively respond to and design Tier 2 interventions? What adjustments do we need to make, if any?
- How do we check to see whether the targeted Tier 2 intervention is working and effective? What assessments are we using to determine the effectiveness of the Tier 2 intervention?

Team Action Steps

Now that you've reflected, identify two strengths in your teacher team practice related to assessment work.

Identify two steps your team will take to deepen your assessment work and when those steps will occur.

Second Helpings © 2027 Solution Tree Press • SolutionTree.com
Visit **go.SolutionTree.com/RTIatWork** to download this free reproducible.

CHAPTER 2

Analyzing the Data to Prepare for Tier 2 Intervention

When you're finishing a delicious meal, you probably reflect on what you might want *just a little more of* to feel truly satisfied. So, you thoughtfully review what you've already eaten, glance around the table to see what's left, and maybe even consider who prepared each dish. Several factors influence what you reach for next. You might consider which dish tasted sweet or savory, or which dish you just couldn't get enough of. While the guests are surveying the table, the hosts are responsible for ensuring the guests get what they need. This mirrors Tier 2 instruction. Tier 1 is like the full meal; it provides all students with access to essential grade-level skills. Tier 2 isn't about repeating the whole meal. It's about getting just the right second helping: targeted support based on what each student still needs to be fully satisfied and successful, or master the essential standards. The teacher team analyzes assessment data—often the end-of-unit assessment—to ensure students are getting the intervention and extension they need.

This chapter describes the moves teacher teams make in analyzing assessment data to plan for student needs, which includes the following.

- Reflecting on the effectiveness of first, best instruction
- Identifying students' misconceptions based on the assessment data to organize students into targeted, skill-based groups
- Determining who delivers instruction
- Determining how long the intervention will last

The Purpose of Analyzing Data

An essential step in the Tier 2 planning process is analyzing assessment data—and let's be honest, data discussions aren't always comfortable. Just like at a traditional potluck, there might be a few dishes you steer clear of because your trust in the chef just isn't quite there yet. Similarly, it takes time for a team to build trust and reach a point where discussing data doesn't feel personal or intimidating, especially when new members may not yet be familiar with what effective data conversations should sound like. In other cases, your team may have no trouble bringing data to the table, but when it's time to review it, you're left with more questions than answers: What should we look at first? How do we talk about student performance productively? What should our next steps be?

That's where a clear data-analysis protocol, or a step-by-step guide to analyzing data, becomes invaluable. A well-designed protocol guides the conversation, keeping the focus on controllable, actionable factors. It ensures that data discussions are collaborative, safe, and centered on solutions. When teams dig into assessments using a shared process, they can uncover student strengths, identify specific skill gaps, and determine appropriate next steps for targeted support.

Ultimately, this analysis clarifies how best to group students and tailor instruction, whether it's intervention or extension, to help every learner move toward proficiency and beyond. It's a critical part of the process, allowing educators to act early and effectively, close learning gaps before they widen, and continue challenging students who are ready for more.

Structured data-discussion processes developed out of school improvement research and professional learning work, including the National School Reform Faculty's (n.d.) collaborative protocols and the thinking routines developed through Harvard Graduate School of Education's Project Zero (Ritchhart, Church, & Morrison, 2011). Over time, these structured approaches have been widely adopted in PLC, RTI, and MTSS frameworks to help teacher teams examine assessment results carefully and decide on targeted instructional next steps.

Research highlights how this structured, systematic approach leads to better outcomes for students and more effective teaching overall. For example, a study by assessment researcher Laura Hamilton and colleagues (2009) finds that when educators consistently analyze student data, their interventions are more focused and lead to stronger academic gains. This is further illustrated in studies by Susan M. Brookhart and James H. McMillan (2020) and Jill Willis, Julie Arnold, and Christopher DeLuca (2023), which both find that the conversations that happen when teacher teams review data and student work, plan instruction based on student misconceptions, and determine next steps clarify for teachers what mastery looks like. Such conversations increase teacher expertise in their content and improve their ability to explain it to students. Better explanations lead to students achieving at higher levels.

This process is effective for all teachers including those who are untraditionally certified or newer to teaching because the collaborative team process increases every teacher's ability to teach well. This supports what we already know about RTI and MTSS: Data-driven decisions make a big difference (Andrade, Bennett, & Cizek, 2019; Goddard, Hoy, & Hoy, 2000; Goodwin & Rouleau, 2022; Hattie, 2023; Skaalvik & Skaalvik, 2007).

Data protocols are a game changer when it comes to supporting students through RTI. Robert J. Marzano (2007) emphasizes data's critical role in driving instructional decisions. It's important that collaborative teacher teams regularly review student performance data to design and adjust interventions that truly meet individual student needs (Mattos et al., 2025).

When schools implement clear data protocols within an RTI or MTSS framework, they're better able to do the following.

- Identify students who are at risk early on, using both academic and behavioral data
- Develop targeted intervention groups tailored to those specific needs
- Monitor student progress to see what's working
- Adjust instruction based on real, up-to-date insights

In *Taking Action*, Mattos and colleagues (2025) explain the importance of analyzing assessment data to form targeted intervention groups based on the specific skill needs identified. They emphasize that these groups should remain flexible, allowing students to move in and out as their assessment results change, ensuring that support is responsive and aligned to each learner's progress. An added benefit to the process of analyzing data and grouping students in this manner is that it gives the teacher clarity on what feedback to give students after they have taken the assessment.

When students understand what they are working toward, they can set goals, track their growth, and stay motivated. Clarity helps them recognize their strengths and focus on areas for improvement. It also allows teachers to give timely, targeted support and celebrate progress along the way. Knowing their learning targets helps students become more confident, responsible, and independent learners. This awareness builds a growth mindset and prepares them for continued success in school and beyond. Chapter 4 goes into more detail on how teams can capitalize on what they learn during their data analysis to cultivate student investment.

Beyond helping with instructional planning, structured data meetings also strengthen collaboration. At the heart of that collaboration is trust. John Hattie's (2023) research identifies collective teacher efficacy as the single most powerful influence on student achievement (with an effect size of 1.57), and trust is the foundation for building it. When educators feel safe and supported, they're more willing to be open about their students' needs, reflect on their own practices, and ask for help when needed (Tschannen-Moran, 2001).

In the context of data discussions, trust is everything. Without it, conversations can feel personal or even judgmental. Teachers might hesitate to speak up about instructional gaps or worry that student performance reflects poorly on their teaching. But when trust exists, teams can shift from a mindset of blame to one of shared problem solving. It becomes less about what *you* did or didn't do and more about what *we* can do together to support every learner.

Building this kind of trust doesn't happen overnight; it takes intentionality. Clear norms, shared expectations, and structured meeting protocols help create a predictable, respectful space for dialogue. As trust grows, teachers begin to value each other's input, lean on each other's strengths, and celebrate collective wins. Kathryn Parker Boudett, Elizabeth A. City, and Richard J. Murnane (2013) emphasize that structured data protocols not only support better decisions, but also foster a culture of continuous improvement. Douglas Fuchs and Lynn S. Fuchs (2006) also find that regular progress monitoring and team-based analysis help pinpoint learning gaps early, allowing schools to act fast and more effectively personalize interventions, especially at Tier 2. When teachers trust one another, these discussions become even more meaningful and impactful.

Schools that use structured data protocols report better use of time and resources. As Sharon V. Kramer (2021) notes in *Charting the Course for Leaders*, these systems help teams stay focused on the students who need support the most and ensure that every strategy is evidence based, timely, and purposeful. In the end, strong collaboration powered by trust and guided by data leads to more confident teachers and more successful students. Teacher efficacy grows as teams act on their data analysis and see students achieve the essential standards.

Data-Analysis Protocol in Action

When engaging in data analysis, selecting the right protocol or guide for the job is essential. While many protocols can guide data conversations, some are more effective and efficient than others. The goal is to find a protocol that not only supports clear and meaningful analysis but also helps teams plan instruction that meets the diverse needs of all students. Effective data analysis must lead to instructional action, or intervention, that causes students to grow and achieve essential standards (Andrade et al., 2019; Brookhart & McMillan, 2020; Ruiz-Primo & Brookhart, 2018).

As you evaluate different templates that might serve as a data-analysis protocol, consider the questions the protocol asks teacher teams to discuss about student performance analysis. For example, the questions on the protocol should emphasize a strengths-based approach, starting with what students know and can do, as shown in the assessment data. It's also important that the protocol highlights the strengths of the Tier 1 instructional practices the teachers used, encouraging teams to reflect on what's working well in their teaching. The strengths the data reveals can help the team uncover the instructional strategies that positively impact student learning and inform Tier 2 interventions that other students can benefit from.

An effective protocol should break down student proficiency in a clear, actionable way, allowing teams to look at proficiency levels student by student, class by class, and learning target by learning target. If the essential standard being measured has an accompanying rubric, data would be broken down by criteria and level on the rubric. This level of detail can help identify students who need additional time and support in specific skill areas, as well as those who are ready for enrichment and extension.

Additionally, a strong data-analysis protocol should drive intentional conversations. The protocol should naturally lead to next steps for planning both intervention and extension, ensuring that instructional decisions are rooted in student needs and based on assessment evidence. Choosing a protocol with these features helps teams stay focused, collaborative, and proactive in their approach to supporting all learners.

Before engaging in a data-analysis protocol with a team, it is important that each teacher first records the performance of students in their own classroom item-analysis sheet. Figure 2.1 (page 38) provides an example template for how an individual teacher can document student performance by assessed standard and organize the results by learning target. Because standards are often complex and

Teacher: Mrs. Blevins

Unit: Expressions and Equations

Standards: 6.EE.1—Write and evaluate numerical expressions involving whole number exponents. **6.EE.2—**Write and solve equations using variables.

Student Name	**Learning Target 1:** 6.EE.1—Write algebraic expressions	**Learning Target 2:** 6.EE.1—Evaluate algebraic expressions	**Learning Target 3:** 6.EE.2—Identify and define variables	**Learning Target 4:** 6.EE.2—Create and solve expressions involving variables
white = proficient; light gray = nearly proficient; dark gray = far from proficient				
Rory B.				
Quincy C.				
Grayson C.				
Catie C.				
Atlas E.				
AmyLee H.				
Matt H.				
Britney R.				
Lennox W.				
Andrew W.				

Figure 2.1: Individual class item analysis.

include multiple skills, breaking assessment questions into specific learning targets provides clearer insight into which components students have mastered and which areas may require additional instruction or support.

In this example, the teacher used a color-coding system (grayscale shown here) to show how students performed. A white box indicates the student was proficient in that learning target, light gray indicates close to proficiency, and dark gray indicates far from proficiency.

In the next step, the grade-level team uses a data-analysis protocol to compile their collective results of student performance. Team members answer a set of questions about the assessment results, uncovering strengths and opportunities for future instruction, and develop their plan for Tier 2 intervention. This protocol, such as the example template in figure 2.2, focuses conversations on student learning and reduces the chance of jumping to conclusions or relying on opinions.

Teacher Name	Learning Target 1:	Learning Target 2:	Learning Target 3:	Learning Target 4:

Data-Analysis Protocol
What are some student strengths? What are some strengths in our teaching strategies?
In what areas did students struggle?
Which assessment items did students most frequently get incorrect? Why? What misconceptions emerged?
What improvements do we need to make to the assessment? To our teaching?
What strategies will we use for intervention and extension considering the misconceptions noted?
How will we group students for interventions? Who will be responsible for interventions, and who will be responsible for extensions?

Source: Adapted from Buffum & Mattos, 2015.

Figure 2.2: Data-analysis protocol.

Visit ***go.SolutionTree.com/RTIatWork*** *for a free reproducible version of this figure.*

To view a detailed example, look ahead to page 44 to see how a grade-level team records their collective percentages of proficiency for each question assessed, then engages in conversations about the data using the question prompts.

By examining trends across the entire team's results, team members identify patterns in student strengths and needs, determine which standards require additional support, and make shared decisions about instructional next steps. When teachers take the time to prepare individually and then come together with a shared purpose, data meetings become focused, efficient, and action oriented.

To make sure their time together truly leads to better outcomes for students, teams should consistently follow four key action steps, described in the next section.

Steps for Successful Data Analysis

A well-planned data analysis session should follow four essential action steps to ensure that teams use their time effectively and make decisions that lead to improved student outcomes.

1. **Enter data prior to the meeting:** Before engaging in the protocol discussion, team members should enter all student data, item by item, into an item-analysis document. This should include each student's name and their performance on every question, aligned with the scoring agreements the team established before administering the assessment. This preparation allows teams to devote their limited meeting time to rich analysis and planning rather than data entry.
2. **Bring the assessments to the table and use student work to drive conversation:** The real value of a protocol lies in the conversations it sparks. Teams should use student work samples alongside the data to analyze performance trends and discuss the effectiveness of the instructional strategies they used. The data-analysis protocol's guiding questions help facilitate meaningful dialogue, allowing teachers to reflect on what worked, identify areas for improvement, and plan targeted next steps. These conversations also help clarify groupings for intervention and extension and determine who will take responsibility for delivering them. Recording the team's thinking in the protocol document builds a foundation for proactive planning and prevention strategies for future learners. If the team consistently spends all of its time entering data, members may start with examining student work from the end-of-unit assessment (and stop entering the data into a spreadsheet).

Team members initially score a small sample (six to eight assessments) of student work together and then identify the most common misconceptions. The instructional intervention planning is based on the identified misconceptions. Teachers score the rest of the work during the meeting, if they have time, or after the meeting as now they have a clearer picture of what to look for in the assessments.

3. **Group students for intervention and extension:** Using the data and student work, teams form groups based on students' specific needs, whether for reteaching essential skills or providing extension. The team also determines what instruction will take place during intervention and extension time, ensuring that each student gets what they need to move forward.
4. **Refer to the proficiency scale and scoring agreements:** Throughout the data analysis process, teams must maintain clarity on what proficiency truly looks like. Team members may realize they didn't all share the same understanding of the rigor required to meet the standard. Revisiting the proficiency scale and scoring agreements ensures that students are placed in the correct groups. Those nearing proficiency may work on reinforcing the targeted skills within the scale's 3.0 content, while students below proficiency may need instruction in prerequisite concepts outlined in the 2.0 content. The clarity a proficiency scale provides will guide purposeful and differentiated intervention planning that meets students where they are and helps them progress toward performing at grade level.

Data Analysis Scenarios

Imagine a team of fourth-grade teachers have just given an end-of-unit assessment and they are at their weekly collaborative team meeting to analyze the results. The assessed items focused on essential comprehension standards of a fiction text and the learning targets, key vocabulary, and prerequisite skills were identified prior to teaching the unit. Additionally, the team used its proficiency scale to create a table of scoring agreements for the assessment they administered and used these agreements to score each student's assessment and place them in the categories of proficiency for each target. The team has already entered their student assessment data from the end-of-unit assessment in their individual teacher item-analysis document they use to prepare for their data-analysis protocol discussion.

This section provides examples of the team's data-analysis protocol work, along with a scripted scenario outlining the team's conversation as team members analyzed the assessment results and collaborated on plans for next steps to determine their response for intervention or extension. Figure 2.3 shows the team's unpacking of standards, using proficiency scales to guide them, that took place before Tier 1 instruction for the unit began.

Standard	Learning Targets (3.0)	Key Academic Vocabulary	Prerequisite Skills and Knowledge (2.0)
RL.4.2— Determine a theme of a story, drama, or poem from details in the text; summarize the text.	I can figure out the theme of a story using clues from the text. I can explain how story details support the theme. I can summarize a story including only the most important parts.	conclusion, key detail, lesson, main idea, message, moral, summary, support, theme	Identify the central message Retell using sequence Recognize character challenges and lessons Record key details
RL.4.3— Describe in depth a character, setting, or event in a story or drama, drawing on specific details in the text.	I can describe a character's traits, feelings, motivations, and actions using evidence. I can describe the setting and how it affects the story. I can explain an important event and how it moves the story forward.	change, character traits, describe, details, event, evidence, influence, mood, motivation, setting	Identify story elements Use descriptive language Understand sequence and cause and effect Locate descriptive evidence

Source for standard: NGA & CCSSO, 2010a.

Figure 2.3: Example of unpacking standards by fourth-grade team.

This process develops clarity for the grade-level team, ensuring that all teachers know their standards well and all students are receiving strong and consistent instruction regardless of the class they are in.

Figure 2.4 shows the team's essential standards scoring agreements for the end-of-unit assessment, again using the proficiency scale to determine their criteria for proficiency.

RL.4.2—Determine a theme of a story, drama, or poem from details in the text; summarize the text.		
Proficient (Success Criteria)	**Close to Proficient**	**Far From Proficient**
• Applies the meaning of academic vocabulary • Uses context clues to identify the theme • Uses text evidence to support the theme • Summarizes the most important events	• Identifies the meaning of academic vocabulary • Identifies text evidence to support a theme • Identifies challenges a character faces • Retells the story in sequence	• Has little to no knowledge of academic vocabulary • Identifies few to no story elements • Identifies few to no character challenges
RL.4.3—Describe in depth a character, setting, or event in a story or drama, drawing on specific details in the text.		
Proficient (Success Criteria)	**Close to Proficient**	**Far From Proficient**
• Applies the meaning of academic vocabulary • Describes a character's motivations, traits, and feelings using text evidence • Explains how the setting affects the story • Explains how important events move the story forward	• Identifies the meaning of academic vocabulary • Identifies story elements • Identifies description words in the text • Identifies cause-and-effect relationships in the text	• Has little to no knowledge of academic vocabulary • Fails to use text to describe characters, settings, or events • Identifies few to no story elements

Source for standard: NGA & CCSSO, 2010a.

Figure 2.4: Example of essential standard scoring agreements by fourth-grade team.

Determining proficiency criteria in advance ensures that the Tier 1 instruction delivered throughout the unit adequately prepares the students for success on the end-of-unit assessment.

Ms. McDowell serves as her fourth-grade team's professional learning team facilitator. Her team has just administered an English language arts (ELA) assessment and has already scored it and entered their data into their individual item-analysis data sheet. The team is now ready to analyze their collective results to begin planning intervention and extension groups.

> ***Ms. McDowell:*** OK, everyone, on today's agenda, we need to review the results of our ELA unit assessment and complete a data-analysis protocol so that we know who needs intervention or extension. Let's get out our students' assessments and bring up our data sheet that shows how students performed on each priority standard we assessed in this unit. Let's identify and record our total number and percentage of students proficient for each item on the assessment.

The team members consult their item-analysis data sheets, shown in figure 2.5. This sheet uses color-coding (grayscale shown here) to easily identify how students performed in each learning target, with shading indicating student proficiency levels with various essential standards. Team members count their total number of proficient scores for each question and report their percentage in the team's data-analysis protocol.

Teacher: Ms. McDowell

Unit: Comprehension of Fiction Text

Student Name	RL.4.2—Summarize	RL.4.2—Theme	RL.4.2—Text Evidence	RL.4.3—Character Traits	RL.4.3—Event Description
white = proficient; light gray = close to proficient; dark gray = far from proficient					
Jane B.					
Nash D.					
Matteo D.					
Jermaine H.					
Blakely M.					
Anya N.					
Jaylen P.					
Malachi R.					
Raelyn Y.					

Source for standard: NGA & CCSSO, 2010a.

Figure 2.5: Example item-analysis data sheet by fourth-grade teacher.

Ms. McDowell counts the total number of white squares for each column, which indicates students who are proficient on that learning target, and converts that number into a percentage. When the teachers complete this process, Ms. McDowell continues to lead the conversation using the questions in the protocol.

Ms. McDowell: Let's begin by discussing what our students did really well.

Ms. Smith: Apart from just a few students, I noticed that most of our students mastered describing characters and events. Our Tier 1 strategies really were effective. I was also really proud of how the students were going back into the text and looking for evidence, especially on the questions that address RL.4.3. Many were using those strategies that we modeled for them in Tier 1. I think we did a great job as a team thinking back to when we taught this unit last year and planning ahead for what students commonly struggled with in past years.

Mr. Yang: I agree, that was very helpful. Looking at everyone's item analyses, it seems our strategy for summarizing text was also effective for many kids. It really helped having them block the paragraphs and write a brief sentence summary for each. Those who didn't use that strategy were the ones who struggled. We have quite a few who are very close to proficient in describing characters. I think they need just a little more practice and they will reach proficiency in no time.

Ms. McDowell: Great. We definitely want to note that in our protocol so that we can refer to this next year when planning for this unit. Now let's look at the areas where most students seemed to struggle. Looking at my item analysis, using text evidence to identify the theme was tricky. Many students missed both questions simply because if they didn't know the theme, it was hard to choose which option provided the best evidence to support the theme.

Mr. Yang: I am seeing that too. I also noticed that if students struggled with the summary, then it was difficult for them to determine the theme.

Ms. Smith: My data reflects the same trend. I have only a few students that need to work on identifying character traits and describing the setting and events, but like Mr. Yang said, with a little more practice, they will get there. Most of my students struggled with theme and evidence.

Ms. McDowell: I noted those areas in our protocol notes. That leads us to our next question: What problems did students struggle with and why? We know that questions students most frequently missed were numbers two and three. Let's look through our assessments and unpack why we think that is.

Ms. Smith: Most of my students struggled with relating the problem and solution to the overall theme of the story. They weren't using their summarizing skills to help them infer the theme.

Mr. Yang: I would agree with that. I also still had a few students raise their hands during the test and ask, "What does theme mean again?" I need to make sure that they really know that academic vocabulary and the concept of theme.

Ms. McDowell: So, do you feel we need to make any adjustments to the assessment or our teaching in general? I personally think that for the text-evidence question, we should change the question type. We made it a short-answer item, and I am wondering whether we should instead include an excerpt from the text and have students highlight the sentence that provides the best evidence and then explain their choice. That will help us really see what connections they are making to the text. Looking at our state assessment item specifications and our state test released items, that is the item type students most typically see. However, we definitely need to see whether students can explain their evidence, as that is the cognitive level required in the standard. The state test will be easier for students if they have done a deeper dive prior to the test.

Ms. Smith: I love that idea. I can help update that change right now. Mr. Yang, do you agree as well?

Mr. Yang: Yes, I think that is a great idea. I felt like the rest of our question types aligned well with the standard. As far as our teaching strategies go, I am going to make sure I create academic vocabulary anchor charts with examples to help students remember words like theme. We also discussed the trend that students who struggled failed to relate characters' problems with the overall theme. Because of that, we should note that students need a strategy for relating the challenges the character faced with what they learned and what the author wants them as readers to learn. In addition, I think students may need more time practicing how to explain the connection between theme and evidence.

Ms. McDowell: Perfect. Our next question on the protocol asks about the strategies we will use for intervention and extension. When we created this unit, we also created a menu of intervention strategies and some extension ideas. Let's bring that document up and see which strategies we need to pull out to meet the needs of our students.

You can see the menu of interventions in figure 2.6. This tool, which the team developed when preparing for Tier 1 instruction, becomes vital when planning

<table>
<tr><th colspan="5">Fourth-Grade ELA Essential Standards Instructional Menu</th></tr>
<tr><th>Standards</th><th>Learning Targets</th><th>Tier 1 Strategies</th><th>Tier 2 Strategies</th><th>Extension Strategies</th></tr>
<tr>
<td>RL.4.2—

Determine a theme of a story, drama, or poem from details in the text; summarize the text.</td>
<td>I can figure out the theme of a story using clues from the text.

I can explain how story details support the theme.

I can summarize a story including only the most important parts.</td>
<td rowspan="2">Anchor Charts: Cocreate a theme chart with examples of common themes.

Text Clue Hunt: After a read-aloud or shared reading, have students highlight or jot down parts of the text that give clues to the message or lesson.

Small Summaries: Students number paragraphs or sections, then write a one-sentence summary for each.

Character Webs: Use graphic organizers that help students link character traits with text evidence and events.

Cause-and-Effect Chain: Use graphic organizers to link one event to what happens next, emphasizing story movement.</td>
<td rowspan="2">Theme Sort with Justification: Give prewritten possible themes and ask students to match them to short passages and explain why using specific story clues.

Sentence Sorting: Have students mix strong and weak text evidence sentences. Students sort sentences based on whether or not they support the theme and explain their reasoning.

Sentence Frames for Summarizing: Provide simple stems like the SWBST (somebody, wanted, but, so, then) frame: "The story is about somebody named ______, who wanted ______. But ______. So ______. Then ______."

Trait-Feeling-Motivation Sort: Provide simple scenarios or story excerpts and have students sort traits, feelings, and motivations with visual cues.

Cause-and-Effect Pairing: Give events and outcomes on cards and have students match them to see how the plot moved forward.</td>
<td rowspan="2">Compare Themes Across Texts: Have students read two stories and explain how the themes are similar or different using text evidence.

Write a Story With a Clear Theme: Challenge students to write a short story where a character learns a lesson and readers can infer the theme.

Write Like the Character: Write a journal entry or letter from the character's point of view, showing their traits and feelings with voice.

Plot Twist Challenge: Have students write an alternate version of the story where the key event didn't happen and explain how it changes the ending.</td>
</tr>
<tr>
<td>RL.4.3—

Describe in depth a character, setting, or event in a story or drama, drawing on specific details in the text.</td>
<td>I can describe a character's traits, feelings, motivations, and actions using evidence.

I can describe the setting and how it affects the story.

I can explain an important event and how it moves the story forward.</td>
</tr>
</table>

Source for standard: NGA & CCSSO, 2010a.

Figure 2.6: Example essential standards instructional menu made by fourth-grade team.

interventions. Teachers often face the challenge of limited time, and having a menu of strategies prepared in advance reduces the stress of planning on the spot. These menus also provide consistency across classrooms, ensuring that all students have access to high-quality interventions and extensions. In addition, they serve as an invaluable support for new teachers who may not yet have the experience or capacity to design interventions independently. With clear menus in place, collaboration is more focused, planning time is more efficient, and every teacher has the tools needed to respond effectively to student needs. The conversation continues. For more about instructional menus, see chapter 4.

Ms. Smith: We know most of our students need support in determining the theme, so I think the theme sort with justification strategy is a great starting point. Students can practice matching a given theme to a passage, then highlight within the passage the evidence that supports the theme.

Mr. Yang: The groups of students who struggled with summarizing can use the SWBST sentence frame to verbalize and write the summary. The trait sorts and the cause-and-effect chains will work great for those students needing intervention in those areas.

Ms. McDowell: Sounds good. For students who need extension, we will give them some voice and choice and let them choose the project on the menu they would like to work on. Our final step is to organize the students into groups. Let's prioritize which skills require intervention first. For example, students must be able to summarize the text first before they can identify the theme and provide evidence.

Mr. Yang: I think that students need to start by describing character, then describing events, which will then help with summarizing. That will lead to identifying the theme and supporting it with evidence.

Ms. McDowell: Perfect. I've recorded our reflections on our protocol.

As the team members engage in conversation, Ms. McDowell records their data and reflections in the data analysis protocol document in figure 2.7.

The team meeting continues, with Ms. McDowell directing team members to begin placing students into groups for targeted Tier 2 intervention using the document in figure 2.8 (page 51).

Unit: *Comprehending fiction text*

Standards:

RL.4.2—*Determine theme in a story, drama, or poem using details from the text; summarize the text.*

RL.4.3—*Describe in depth a character, setting, or event in a story or drama, drawing on specific details in the text.*

Teacher Name	Learning Target 1: RL.4.2—Summarize	Learning Target 2: RL.4.2—Theme	Learning Target 3: RL.4.2—Text Evidence	Learning Target 4: RL.4.3—Character Traits	Larning Target 5: RL.4.3—Event Description
Ms. McDowell	71%	53%	47%	88%	94%
Ms. Smith	76%	47%	35%	94%	94%
Mr. Yang	65%	41%	47%	88%	88%

What are some student strengths? What are some strengths in our teaching strategies?

Most students mastered describing characters and events. Students who were successful on RL.4.3 were using strategies for text evidence. The summarizing strategy for blocking paragraphs and jotting a sentence to summarize each was effective for most students. There are many students who are very close to proficiency who may need just a little more practice.

In what areas did students struggle?

The students who struggled with text evidence also struggled with finding the theme. The students who struggled with summarizing struggled with theme as well. The few who need to work on describing traits and settings need more time to practice. Theme and evidence are where most students need support.

Which assessment items did students most frequently get incorrect? Why? What misconceptions emerged?

Questions 2 and 3 were most often missed. Many students asked what theme means, showing that they struggled with academic vocabulary. Students need to use the summary to help them identify the theme and text evidence.

What improvements do we need to make to the assessment? To our teaching?

Change the short answer question for text evidence to highlighting within an excerpt. Then allow students to explain the evidence while referring to the text. For instruction, we need to make sure we intentionally teach academic vocabulary.

Figure 2.7: Example data-analysis protocol by fourth-grade team.

continued ▶

What strategies will we use for intervention and extension considering the misconceptions noted? *Intervention strategies: Theme justification and sort, then highlight evidence within the passage, use an SWBT sentence frame to support summarizing, character trait sort, and cause-and-effect chains for describing events* *Extensions: Voice and choice menu to allow students to apply the standard at a deeper level, such as comparing themes across texts, plot twist challenge to apply describing events, or a character journal entry to reinforce the specific character traits*
How will we group students for interventions? Who will be responsible for interventions and who will be responsible for extensions? *Intervention needs to start with students describing character then events, which will support their summarizing skills.* *Students then move to summarizing, then theme and evidence.* *Ms. Smith: Describing events* *Mr. Yang: Summarizing* *Ms. McDowell: Identifying theme and evidence* *Mr. Jax: Describing character traits, motivations, and feelings* *Ms. Hill: Extension*

Ms. McDowell: Everyone, look at your individual item analysis and start plugging students in where they need more support. We will use our support staff for two of the groups. Ms. Smith, you can work with the students in the "describe events" group and Mr. Yang, you can take the "summarizing" group. I will meet with the "theme and evidence" group. Put an asterisk by the names of students who were far from proficient in each learning target. And a diamond by the names of students who were close to proficient. We will make sure to structure our groups so that students who are close to proficiency get more practice and students who need more intensive support receive a scaffolded small-group lesson.

Figure 2.8 shows the results of the team placing students into the various targeted intervention categories.

Ms. McDowell: All students are now placed into groups. We will plan for two weeks of intervention and extension for thirty minutes. We will bring our progress-monitoring data, based on our exit slips or a mini quiz, to update our

Essential Standards	Describing character traits, motivations, and feelings	Describing events	Summarizing	Identifying theme or evidence	Extension group
Teacher Responsible	Mr. Jax	Ms. Smith	Mr. Yang	Ms. McDowell	Ms. Hill
Students	Jane* Sam* Blaine* Monica* Malachi*	Teverlee△ Cali△ Adrianna△ Kade△	Quinlyn* Blaine* Matteo* Cadence* Luis◊ Rijay◊ Jace◊ Jennifer◊ Matthew◊ Erik◊ Jaylen◊ Alex◊ Cohen◊	Jane* Anya* Blakely* Ragnar* Lillian* Jada* Jorge◊ Jessa◊ Raelyn◊ Oliver◊ Liam◊ Elliot◊ Jaime◊	Nash Abigail Jillian Tony Hudson Colton Angel Norra Octavio Pearl Rickson Jermain Liam Jarrod Anna David

Figure 2.8: Example Tier 2 groupings by fourth-grade team.

groups at the end of the two weeks. Before we begin intervention, are there any questions about the learning targets or scoring agreements?

Ms. Smith: I feel like our team has a good understanding, but I will make sure to meet with our support staff, Mr. Jax and Ms. Hill, so they understand what students should be able to do. I think we should also plan to meet with students to give feedback on the assessment and let them know the evidence they need to show in their intervention to prove mastery.

Mr. Yang: Good point. I think I will confer with students this afternoon. Also, Ms. McDowell, our groups are fairly large. What is your plan to support both the students who are nearly proficient and those who are still far from proficient?

Ms. McDowell: Great question! Since I know the nearly proficient students need a little more practice, I will start with a minilesson with the whole group. Then, I'll release the nearly proficient students to complete a practice activity while keeping the students needing support with me for more guided practice. Finally, when I give them their task, I will check in with the other students and give feedback on their progress.

Mr. Yang: Great idea. I will structure my intervention group the same way.

Ms. McDowell: Perfect! So, to sum up, we will all make sure to follow up with the students to give feedback on the assessment, then let them know what groups they will be working in. Great job, everyone. To end, let's quickly review our overall results and progress toward proficiency. Count your total number of proficient students in each learning target, the total number of students who are close or developing, and the total number of students who aren't there yet. Again, we will update these numbers at the end of our intervention cycle.

The team documents proficiency levels of all students using the report shown in figure 2.9. As the students provide evidence of mastery, the team continuously updates the document to reflect the most current results. Tracking the total number of students who reach proficiency on each grade-level standard throughout the year allows the team to monitor collective progress toward guaranteed learning for all. This ongoing record helps teams evaluate the impact of their instruction, identify patterns across units, and make timely adjustments to ensure more students reach and sustain proficiency over time.

Learning Target	Proficient	Developing	Not Yet	Total Percent Proficient
Summary	38	9	4	75%
Theme	18	18	15	35%
Evidence	16	12	23	31%
Character Traits	46	5	0	90%
Event Description	47	2	2	92%

Figure 2.9: Example proficiency levels summary by fourth-grade team.

This process of analyzing data isn't about checking a box or filling out another form. It's about building clarity and shared responsibility for student learning. When teams consistently follow these steps, the process becomes predictable because it helps move from simply looking at scores to taking meaningful instructional action in Tier 2 interventions. Once that structure is in place, the real work is continuously refining and strengthening the process with each new cycle of instruction and intervention.

Are You Ready?

Talking about student data and student work from common assessments is one of the most important steps when planning Tier 2 interventions. These conversations help the team focus on what the data indicates and give everyone a chance to think about what might be affecting student performance. When teachers take time to spot patterns and trends, it helps them better understand what students need and encourages growth as educators. These discussions are even more powerful when there's a clear process to follow. That's where a data-analysis protocol comes in because it keeps the conversation on track and ensures everyone looks at the same things in the same way.

Using a data-analysis protocol is so important because it brings consistency and clarity to the table. It helps teams stay focused on facts, not guesses, and makes it easier to figure out next steps for instruction. It also makes sure every student's data gets the attention it deserves, not just the ones who are struggling the most. With a strong protocol in place, everyone is on the same page, and it becomes easier to make smart, student-centered decisions. In the end, it's all about making sure teams spend time in ways that truly support student growth. After your team has assessed your readiness, use the reflection questions in the reproducible tool "Pause and Take Action: Chapter 2" (page 54).

Once the team has reviewed the data and gained an overall understanding of what each student needs, the next step is moving from analysis to action. The next chapter will guide teams in delivering Tier 2 interventions, connecting the insights they gain from the protocol directly to targeted instruction that meets students where they are and helps them make measurable progress. This sets the stage for turning careful analysis into meaningful, effective teaching.

Pause and Take Action: Chapter 2

Consider the following questions to determine your teacher team's next data-analysis actions.

- Do we prioritize time to analyze data as a team? If so, what has allowed our team to protect that time? If not, what might we do to make it to a priority?
- How clear is our team about proficiency levels and scoring agreements? Do we have a process for developing learning progression or proficiency scales and scoring agreements?
- Do we have a data-analysis protocol template? If so, what adjustments might we make to that protocol and template? If not, where will we begin?
- Do we have a shared data document to input data? If so, how is it working? If not, what kind of data tracking might be best for us?
- How do we currently group students? To what extent do we organize groups by level of understanding, as indicated by common assessment evidence?
- Does our grouping include specific insights that indicate student strengths and areas of growth in the essential standards? Are we able to identify students who are proficient, close to proficient, and far from proficient?
- To what extent is our team having conversations about stand-out results or intentionally identifying instructional practices that have shown results?
- Is our teacher team clear on its collective role to provide additional support to students? Do team members embrace finding solutions to leading Tier 2 intervention or do they tend to want to send students to someone else or find a program for help on grade-level essentials? How do we continue to clarify that role and sustain effective collaboration?

Team Action Steps

Now that you've reflected, identify two of your strengths in your teacher team practice related to data analysis.

Identify two next steps your team will take to deepen their data analysis and when those steps will occur.

Second Helpings © 2027 Solution Tree Press • SolutionTree.com
Visit **go.SolutionTree.com/RTIatWork** to download this free reproducible.

CHAPTER 3

Designing Instruction for Tier 2 Interventions and Extensions

Planning effective Tier 2 interventions is a lot like trying to recreate a delicious, complex meal. Imagine sitting down to a dish so rich and perfectly balanced that every bite feels like a work of art. Naturally, you ask for the recipe, hoping to replicate the magic in your own kitchen. But once you have it, you realize the recipe alone isn't enough. You're missing the tools, the practice, and the deeper understanding behind each step. To truly master it, you'd need to study the techniques, see them in action, and, ideally, learn directly from the chef.

Tier 2 planning works the same way. It's not just about identifying the right "ingredients," like targeted skills or strategies; it's also about understanding how and when to use them with precision. Just as cooking a great meal requires intention and expertise, so does designing interventions that meet students where they are and move them forward. It takes more than a plan on paper; it takes collaborative learning, refined practice, and thoughtful execution.

In this chapter, we begin to dig into the design and delivery of the instruction itself. We unpack how to build clear Tier 2 planners aligned to specific standards, how to embed gradual release, and how to intentionally plan both intervention and extension before the unit even begins. Realistic classroom scenarios demonstrate what effective Tier 2 instruction looks and sounds like in real time. By combining thoughtful planning with real-life examples of instruction in action, this chapter closes the gap between theory and practice, giving teams the clarity and confidence to implement Tier 2 support with purpose and precision.

The Purpose of Instructional Design for Tier 2

Planning strong Tier 1 instruction takes a lot of time, teamwork, and intention. Teachers work hard to create engaging, standards-based lessons, adjust for different learning needs, and check for understanding. But when it comes to Tier 2, planning can feel overwhelming, especially with limited time, staffing, and resources.

Tier 2 plays a crucial role in supporting students who aren't quite getting there with Tier 1 alone. Recognizing that Tier 2 should look and feel different is a powerful mindset shift. Tier 2 isn't just a repeat of Tier 1; it requires targeted, skill-specific instruction based on student data. That means using new strategies, providing different materials, and keeping a close eye on progress, all while continuing to manage the core classroom. Tier 1 is designed for all learners, but when some students need more, we have to zoom in and get specific.

Tier 2 isn't about reteaching the whole lesson; it's about asking, "Why is this student struggling? Where is their misconception?" and planning instruction that targets that exact need. Maybe it's fluency, maybe it's vocabulary, or maybe students need help breaking down word problems or understanding text structure. Whatever it is, teachers use that information to plan focused targeted group lessons that meet students where they are. These group lessons rely on clear modeling, guided practice, and intentional scaffolds like sentence stems, visual organizers, decodable texts, or manipulatives. Teachers choose tools that support the specific skill they're addressing.

Tier 2 also gives teachers a chance to build deeper relationships with students. In a smaller group, you get to really know how they think, what motivates them, and where they shine. That connection helps you build lessons that are not only supportive but also engaging. You can tap into students' interests, offer choices, and celebrate quick wins that build confidence. The intention is not just to fill academic gaps; it's to help students believe in themselves as learners.

Progress monitoring is another key piece and one that's easy to overlook. But without regular check-ins, you won't know if the intervention is working. It doesn't need to be complex, as just a quick weekly or mid-instruction check on the specific skill targeted can be sufficient. With consistent data, you can adjust instruction, intensify support, and celebrate progress.

Marzano (2009) emphasizes that effective interventions must be both targeted and systematic, noting that when teachers align instruction to specific student needs, achievement gains can be significant. In fact, Robert J. Marzano, Debra J. Pickering, and Jane E. Pollock (2001) find that using focused instructional strategies, such as identifying similarities and differences, summarizing, and using nonlinguistic representations, can produce substantial effect sizes on student learning. These findings underscore why Tier 2 should not simply mirror Tier 1 but instead deliver carefully chosen strategies that directly address gaps that data reveals.

And remember, Tier 2 is meant to be temporary. The goal is to give students the right support so they can confidently achieve the essential standard. That's why teachers need a clear plan for targeted skills and an exit strategy or assessment check for proficiency from the start.

When educators approach Tier 2 with purpose, making it focused, data informed, and relationship driven, it becomes a powerful tool for equity. It's not just intervening—it's empowering. By giving students what they need, exactly when they need it, Tier 2 support helps them grow and thrive alongside their peers.

Tier 2 Intervention and Extension in Action

The hardest part about planning Tier 2 interventions is making them distinct from your Tier 1 approaches. While Tier 1 instruction is designed for all students, Tier 2 requires targeted support that often looks and feels different. Interventions at this level are frequently more hands on, scaffolded, and broken down into simpler, more manageable steps so students can master specific skills. The following sections outline two examples of planning Tier 2 interventions in ELA and mathematics, two areas that strongly influence student performance across other content areas. These examples illustrate how intentional, skill-specific support can help students close gaps and thrive alongside their peers.

Intervention in ELA

One of the most effective ways to set Tier 2 instruction apart from Tier 1 in ELA is by intentionally using scaffolds like graphic organizers, sentence stems, and other high-level instructional strategies to target the missing skills. These tools help make complex tasks more manageable for students who need extra support and give them the structure they need to practice academic thinking.

Graphic organizers are especially powerful in Tier 2. For example, using a character map during a fiction comprehension intervention helps students organize their thoughts about character traits, motivations, and changes over time. Organizers like story maps, sequence charts, or cause-and-effect diagrams help students break down and visualize the structure of the text. A ready-made resource that supports this work is the book *Mining Complex Text, Grades 6–12* by Diane Lapp, Thomas DeVere Wolsey, Karen D. Wood, and Kelly Johnson. This book provides practical, classroom-tested graphic organizers, such as the Search and Find Board, specifically designed to help students unpack dense academic texts. These tools guide learners in organizing information, identifying key ideas, and analyzing structure, which are key skills that struggling readers often need to strengthen.

Sentence stems are also a helpful scaffold for students who may struggle with the oral language structures necessary to express their thoughts in an organized manner. For example, using stems like "At first, the character felt __________ but then __________" or "One problem the character faced was __________ because __________" supports language development while reinforcing comprehension using text evidence.

Targeted strategies like repeated reading for fluency, guided close reads with annotation, and chunking text to retell can make Tier 2 lessons more interactive and meaningful. These strategies are carefully chosen to match the skill focus, provide more immediate feedback, and allow more active practice than Tier 1.

Figure 3.1 provides grade-level examples designed to support Tier 2 intervention in high-leverage ELA standards. Each strategy scaffolds the skill into clear, manageable procedural steps, helping students move toward mastery. These supports guide learners from foundational skills to more complex comprehension skills.

Guiding students through clear procedural steps and intentionally breaking down the process provide the structured support they need to build accuracy and automaticity. Over time, this repeated, scaffolded practice helps students internalize the skill so they can apply it independently and efficiently. The goal is to accelerate progress so students can perform as close to grade-level expectations as possible, as quickly as possible.

Metacognitive strategies are also essential for supporting reading interventions, particularly for students who struggle with comprehension. One highly effective strategy is the use of think-alouds, where teachers model their internal thought processes while reading a text. By verbalizing questions like, "What does the author mean here?" or "This part is confusing, let me reread it," teachers demonstrate how proficient readers monitor their understanding, make predictions, and clarify meaning. As students begin to internalize these strategies, they are better able to pause, reflect, and self-correct when reading independently. Teaching students to practice metacognitive techniques such as summarizing after each paragraph,

Skill Focus	Tier 2 Strategy	Tier 2 Strategy Explained
Decoding words in context	Cut-up sentences	Write a decodable sentence on a sentence strip; then cut each word apart and mix them around. The student puts the sentence back together, rereading each word as they go.
	Sentence pyramids	The student writes or types a decodable sentence, adding one word to each line to create a pyramid. The The cat The cat sat The cat sat on The cat sat on the The cat sat on the mat.
Comprehending story elements in fiction texts	Somebody-wanted-but-so-then hunt	The student highlights the text to hunt for SWBST evidence, then fills out the graphic organizer to map the story. The student uses the SWBST organizer to verbally retell the story.
Comprehending main ideas and details in nonfiction texts	Main idea detective	The student highlights the headings of each section or the first sentence to identify the main idea. Then, the student highlights two supporting details in a different color.
	Block and jot	The student practices blocking out sections of text and jots down a short, five-word summary about each section.
	Deconstructing paragraphs	The student receives a content-heavy paragraph, then circles repeated words or phrases, underlines verbs that show what is happening, and answers what the author is mostly saying about the topic. The student develops a main idea statement and includes two relevant details.

Figure 3.1: Tier 2 instructional strategies for ELA interventions.

questioning the author's purpose, or identifying unfamiliar vocabulary fosters deeper engagement with complex texts (Calderón, 2011). Over time, these habits strengthen reading stamina, critical thinking, and overall confidence in navigating academic content.

In Tier 2, every minute counts, so the instruction needs to be highly focused, scaffolded, and engaging. Once initial Tier 2 instruction is underway, the next step is to monitor student progress closely using informative assessments. This ongoing progress monitoring shows whether the intervention is effectively addressing each student's needs and whether adjustments are necessary. By regularly tracking growth in key ELA skills, teachers can identify students who may need more intensive targeted support (Tier 3) or different strategies. Growth tracking also guides decisions about groupings, instructional focus, and pacing, ensuring that each student continues to move forward. By planning with these tools in mind, teachers make instruction more accessible and successful for students who need just a bit more support to grow.

Intervention in Mathematics

A key part of strong Tier 2 mathematics intervention is building number sense. When students have a solid sense of numbers, they become more confident, flexible thinkers, which makes problem solving and reasoning much easier. Simple daily routines like number talks, choral counting, or estimation activities are great ways to strengthen these skills. For instance, asking students to find all the ways to make twelve helps them break numbers apart and see part-whole relationships, skills that are foundational for more complex mathematics later on.

Mathematics games, such as those listed in figure 3.2, are great tools for Tier 2. They boost engagement, build fluency, and give students repeated practice in a fun, low-stress way. Games like Race to 100 for place value, Multiplication War for fact fluency, or Cover Up for composing and decomposing numbers let students explore mathematical concepts while staying focused on their intervention goals. Built-in time for discussion and reflection helps deepen understanding and encourages metacognition.

Using mathematics learning games in Tier 2 intervention for upper grades can make a big difference in how students engage with and understand mathematics. Instead of drilling problems in the same old way, games like Equation Match-Up make solving linear equations more interactive and visual, helping students see the connection between an equation and its solution. Integer War gives students repeated practice with integer operations in a way that feels more like a card game than a mathematics assignment, and Slope Showdown challenges them to quickly calculate and explain slope using graphs, tables, or coordinate points. The games listed in figure 3.3 (page 62) not only boost fluency and confidence, they also encourage mathematics talk and strategic thinking, which are key parts of what makes Tier 2 support effective and fun.

Another important strategy is using the concrete-representational-abstract (CRA) framework approach, illustrated in figure 3.4 (page 62). This means starting with

Game	Focus Skill	Materials Needed	How to Play
Race to 100	Place value, counting	Two dice, 100 chart, counters or crayons	Players take turns rolling dice, adding the total to their score, and covering that number on the 100 chart. The first to reach one hundred wins. Players discuss their strategy.
Multiplication War	Multiplication fact fluency	Deck of cards, face cards removed	Each player flips two cards and multiplies them. The player with the highest product wins the round. If there's a tie, students play again. The game continues until cards run out.
Cover Up	Composing and decomposing numbers	Game board with numbers (such as a 10-frame or grid), two dice, counters	Players roll two dice, find and cover combinations to make a target number (for example, ten). They take turns until the board is full. Players discuss their combinations.
Make 12 (number combinations)	Number bonds, part-whole thinking	12-frame, counters, number cards	Players draw a number card. Using counters, they show all the ways to make twelve with that number. For example, if card reads 7, a player could show 7 + 5. Players share their different combinations.

Figure 3.2: Mathematics games to support Tier 2 intervention in elementary grades.

hands-on materials like base 10 blocks or counters (concrete), moving to drawings or visual models (representational), and then finally using numbers and symbols (abstract). For example, when teaching subtraction with regrouping, students might first model with blocks, then draw the equation out, and finally solve with the standard algorithm. This progression helps students really understand the *why* behind mathematics, not just memorize steps.

Game	Focus Skill	Materials Needed	How to Play
Equation Match-Up	Linear equations	Index cards with equations and solutions	Create pairs of cards, one with a linear equation (for example, 3x − 5 = 10) and one with the solution (x = 5). Players match them and explain their reasoning.
Integer War	Integer operations (add, subtract, multiply, divide)	Deck of integer cards (positive and negative values)	Each player draws two cards and completes a chosen operation. The highest result wins the round. Play continues until the deck runs out.
Slope Showdown	Finding slope from graphs, tables, or points	Graph cards, sets of coordinates, dry-erase boards	Show a graph, table, or two coordinate points. Players race to calculate the slope and explain how they found it. Players earn points for accuracy and speed.

Figure 3.3: Mathematics games to support Tier 2 intervention in secondary grades.

Stage	Description	Example (adding 23 + 15)	Materials or Tools
Concrete	Students use *physical objects* to model the mathematical problem or concept.	Use base 10 blocks to show two tens plus three ones and one ten plus five ones.	Base 10 blocks, counters, linking cubes
Representational	Students draw *pictures or visual models* to represent the mathematics problem or concept.	Draw tens rods and ones dots to model the numbers.	Paper, place value charts, number lines
Abstract	Students use *numbers and symbols* to solve problems without models.	Solve using standard algorithm: 23 + 15 = 38.	Pencil and paper, mental math

Source: National Center on Intensive Intervention, 2016.

Figure 3.4: CRA framework progression.

Visual models and graphic organizers are particularly effective in supporting student thinking during Tier 2 mathematics interventions. Tools like number lines, 10-frames, part-part-whole diagrams, and place value charts give students something concrete to work with, helping them organize their thinking and solve problems with more confidence. But they only work if educators teach students how and when to use them, so modeling their use and providing plenty of practice are key.

Another significant piece of Tier 2 mathematics is building students' metacognitive skills. Many struggling learners tend to follow procedures without really understanding the *why* behind them. And while steps and formulas are useful, they aren't enough on their own. We want students thinking flexibly, asking themselves questions like, "Does this make sense?" or "Is there another way to solve this?" Modeling and facilitating that kind of reflection verbally and in writing builds deeper understanding and helps students take ownership of their learning. In their book *Mathematic Strategies for Tier 1 and Tier 2 Interventions in a PLC at Work*, Sarah Schuhl, Mona Toncheff, Jennifer Deinhart, and Brian Buckhalter (2025) dive deeper into Tier 2 strategies for mathematical concepts and provide in-depth insights into specific strategies that provide students with just-in-time interventions to close gaps in mathematics.

Just like in ELA, progress monitoring in mathematics is essential. Quick exit tickets, miniassessments, or even informal observations provide the data teachers need to make timely adjustments. If something's not working, a teacher shifts, maybe trying a new scaffold, reteaching differently, or using a different visual model. When teachers use these high-leverage strategies intentionally and consistently, Tier 2 mathematics intervention becomes a powerful way to close gaps and move students to grade-level expectations.

Extension

When educators think about Tier 2, they usually picture students who need extra help, but what about those who've already mastered the basics and are ready for a deeper challenge? That's where extension comes in, and there is a reason it is the focus of the fourth critical question of a PLC (DuFour et al., 2024). Extension isn't about giving students more of the same work; it's about helping them stretch their thinking, apply what they know in new ways, and stay engaged. It can look like giving them a complex problem to solve, encouraging them to make real-world connections, or letting them explore a topic more creatively. In ELA, this could mean asking students who have mastered summarizing a text to analyze multiple sources on the same topic and synthesize a cohesive argument. Additionally, students could write from the perspective of a character, applying textual evidence to support complex reasoning. In mathematics, extension might involve asking students who can solve standard linear equations to model a real-world situation using a system of equations. They might also explore patterns and relationships in data to make predictions, which requires students to apply the same concept but in a more complex context. By thoughtfully designing extension tasks, teachers ensure that students are challenged cognitively, deepen their understanding, and see the relevance of the standard in new, engaging ways.

Unfortunately, these opportunities often get pushed aside. Intervention time is limited, and schools naturally prioritize students who need support. If we don't make room for extension, however, students who are ready to go further can become bored or disengaged. One of the benefits of planning extensions for Tier 2 is that they can be prepared before instruction even begins, allowing teachers to have meaningful challenges ready for students who demonstrate readiness. This proactive approach saves time during intervention sessions and ensures that all learners receive targeted, purposeful opportunities to stretch their thinking, deepen understanding, and engage with grade-level standards in new and meaningful ways. Tier 2 instruction should challenge *all* students, not just those catching up (DuFour et al., 2024). That means using data to identify learners who are ready for more and being just as intentional about planning for their growth.

Students are most motivated when work feels both meaningful and challenging (Tomlinson, 2014). When teachers give students voice and choice, whether that's having them choose how they show what they've learned or digging into something they care about, they feel more invested. These kinds of tasks not only deepen understanding but also develop executive functioning skills like planning and time management, which students need for long-term success. Another form of extension is to have every student choose a project. The teacher might create options and a structure or the students might be able to co-construct a project. As students show mastery of essential standards, they engage in their extension project. This creates meaning for students and lessens the design work for teachers.

Tier 2 extension also plays a role in equity. Sometimes students who consistently achieve higher levels, especially those from underrepresented groups, aren't formally identified for gifted programs. Embedding enrichment opportunities into small groups ensures they don't get overlooked and continue to grow. In the end, it all comes down to this: Every student deserves the chance to grow. Tier 2 isn't just about catching students up; it's about pushing every learner forward, wherever they are.

Intervention and Extension Menus

A common challenge teams experience is knowing what instruction to plan for students once they are in their intervention or extension groups. So much of the teacher team's time and energy went into teaching the essential standards the first time around. This is where the proficiency scale and prerequisite skills come back into play. The data analysis reveals knowledge gaps that hinder students' abilities to reach proficiency, and their intervention is the opportunity to slow down and solidify those missing skills, providing more time to deeply learn the most essential standards. As teams collaborate and plan their units of instruction and review their proficiency scales, developing an intervention and extension menu for each unit can help teachers prepare for focused, hands-on activities that reinforce the grade-level standard. By following these four steps, teams can develop a working document that outlines instructional strategies for Tier 1 instruction as well as Tier 2 intervention and extension activities.

1. **Choose the essential standards that will be the focus of your unit:** A unit of instruction may focus on one or a few essential standards that are closely related. There will usually be other standards (often supporting) to teach. However, teams ensure the unit teaches each essential standard deeply and that the team understands the goal of what students should be able to do by the end of the unit.
2. **Plan Tier 1 instructional strategies:** Any instructional unit should guarantee that all students receive consistent, high-quality instruction from every teacher on the team. Collaborating on Tier 1 instructional strategies is key. Often, teacher teams spend the bulk of their time discussing what they plan on teaching and not enough time planning how. It's in those how conversations that teachers can ensure students are able to get high-quality instruction to move toward and prove proficiency through Tier 1. When planning Tier 1 strategies, teachers should focus on whole-class strategies such as anchor charting, modeling, teacher think-alouds, cooperative learning, and independent practice application to give all students the best opportunity to prove mastery.
3. **Plan Tier 2 instructional strategies:** When planning Tier 2 interventions, teachers must focus on the specific learning targets students need additional support with. Activities should be hands on, broken into manageable steps, and include just-right scaffolds like sentence starters, graphic organizers, and manipulatives. Smaller, targeted

group settings allow for immediate feedback and support, which are gradually removed as students build independence and move closer to mastery. Tier 2 must be something different from Tier 1 instruction.

Teaching metacognitive strategies is also key and includes modeling how to self-monitor, ask questions, and reflect using think-alouds and guided discussions. Keep students engaged through multimodal activities such as mathematics manipulatives, reading storyboards, or movement-based vocabulary games to support diverse learning needs.

Remember that just because a strategy is labeled Tier 2 doesn't mean it should only be used during intervention time. The most effective Tier 1 classrooms are proactive and responsive; teachers flexibly pull in Tier 2 menu strategies when whole-class or small-group data shows a need. This mindset of prevention over remediation helps strengthen core instruction and ensures fewer students fall behind in the first place. By embedding high-leverage supports early and often, teachers reduce the number of students who require intensive interventions later, making their systems more efficient and equitable for all learners.

4. **Plan extension activities:** Planning Tier 2 extension activities for students who have mastered grade-level skills requires a focused and strategic approach. Rather than assigning more of the same, the goal is to deepen understanding, promote critical thinking, and foster independence. Teacher teams should incorporate voice and choice, allowing students to explore interests and choose how they demonstrate understanding. Differentiation through tiered assignments ensures all students engage with the same content at varying levels of complexity. Crosscurricular connections, peer collaboration, and opportunities for student-led learning further enrich instruction. Digital tools and enrichment platforms can support self-paced, challenging tasks, while structured reflection and metacognitive strategies help students monitor their growth and learning process. Intentional extension planning ensures advanced learners remain engaged, challenged, and empowered in their academic journey.

As teacher teams develop and refine instructional menus, these tools evolve into dynamic, living documents that provide lasting value year after year. Over time, as educators collaboratively implement and reflect on instruction, they gain deeper insights into common areas of student misunderstanding and identify effective strategies for both intervention and extension. This continuous refinement process not only enhances instructional quality but also supports the creation of a guaranteed and viable curriculum in which all students have equitable access to essential content and high-quality instruction, regardless of the teacher or classroom.

A significant advantage of maintaining and using these instructional menus is the clarity and consistency they provide across teams. For new team members, these resources eliminate much of the uncertainty that can come with lesson planning and targeted instruction. Instead of relying on isolated efforts, new educators can enter the collaborative space with a strong foundation, supported by proven instructional strategies and aligned expectations, leading to more effective and cohesive teaching practices. Figures 3.5 (page 68) and 3.6 (page 69) provide examples of instructional menus for third-grade ELA and eighth-grade mathematics, respectively.

Taking the time to plan an instructional menu before a unit begins gives the team clarity on the instruction and ensures they have ready-to-use strategies aligned to each standard. This proactive planning allows teachers to respond efficiently to student needs, providing timely interventions without scrambling during the unit or falling into planning interventions that include more of the same type of instruction. By anticipating where students may struggle or excel, teams can save valuable time, maximize instructional impact, and ensure that all learners receive targeted, meaningful support from the very start.

Instructional Design for Groups

Having a menu of activities is only as effective as the teaching that accompanies it. In an RTI system, the responsibility for administering Tier 2 interventions is the teacher team. Other staff members may be able to support, but the teacher team is in the best position and has the expertise to deliver additional support on grade-level essential standards or Tier 2 intervention. These educators work collaboratively to deliver targeted group instruction, monitor student progress, and adjust interventions based on data, ensuring that each student receives the support they need to succeed. It is important that the teacher delivering the intervention has a framework to follow to ensure that students are given the targeted instruction that will lead to mastery of the essential standards.

Figure 3.7 (page 71) provides an organization framework for the intervention. Following the gradual release of responsibility model (Pearson & Gallagher, 1983), this planner embeds intentional modeling, guided practice, and opportunities for application and transfer. Having a detailed planner ensures that intervention instruction is explicit and purposeful, keeping the focus on providing additional time and targeted practice for students who need it most. By embedding the gradual

Standard	Learning Targets	Tier 1 Strategies	Tier 2 Strategies	Extension Strategies
RL.3.1—Ask and answer questions to demonstrate understanding of a text, referring explicitly to the text as the basis for the answers.	I can ask and answer questions about a story and use the text to support my answers.	Cocreate anchor charts with students that explain the standard and include academic vocabulary and examples of how to apply the skill. **RL.3.1**—Ask students to highlight evidence within the text when answering questions. **RL.3.2**—Have students use SWBST as a verbal and written summarizing strategy.	Create an academic vocabulary matching game. **RL.3.1**—Present a text evidence matching game. **RL.3.2**—Chunk paragraphs and introduce the five-word summary reading strategy. **RL.3.2**—Demonstrate how to use a summary flowchart organizer.	Create an academic vocabulary bingo card. **RL.3.1**—Have students write higher-order *why* and *how* questions for their peers that require specific text evidence to answer. **RL.3.1**—Develop an evidence-sorting activity where students provide multiple pieces of text evidence (some relevant, some not) and have other students match them to corresponding questions.
RL.3.2—Recount stories and determine the central message, lesson, or moral.	I can retell a story and explain the lesson or message the author wants me to learn.	**RL.3.2**—Task students with connecting what the character learns to what the author wants readers to learn. **W.3.3**—Supply mentor texts for students to study how authors craft beginnings, middles, and ends of narratives.	**RL.3.2**—Have students color-code story elements using highlighters within a passage. **RL.3.2**—Have students cut and sequence events. **RL.3.2**—Ask students to make a list of common morals or lessons using familiar stories.	**RL.3.2**—Have students write a new ending that teaches a different (but related) lesson and explain how the change affects the central message. **RL.3.2**—Have students read two folktales or fables from different cultures and compare their themes or morals. **RL.3.2**—Ask students to design a poster or digital presentation that illustrates the story's theme with quotes, images, and a personal reflection.
W.3.3—Write narratives to develop real or imagined experiences or events.	I can write a story with a clear beginning, middle, and end and use details to bring it to life.	**W.3.3**—Cowrite a class narrative with students to serve as an example. **W.3.3**—Chunk the narrative into smaller sections (introduction, each event and supporting details, and conclusion). Model only that section and have students independently apply that section to their own narratives.	**W.3.3**—Show how to use paragraph frames for introductions, events, and closings. **W.3.3**—Have students develop a bank of ideas for characters, settings, common problems characters face, and practical solutions.	**W.3.3**—Have students rewrite a familiar story from another character's perspective, using narrative techniques like inner thoughts and dialogue.

Source for standard: NGA & CCSSO, 2010a.

Figure 3.5: Grade 3 ELA essential standards instructional menu.

Standard	Learning Targets	Tier 1 Strategies	Tier 2 Strategies	Extension Strategies
8.EE.C.7— Solve linear equations in one variable. Solve linear equations in one variable, including equations with rational number coefficients and solutions requiring the use of the distributive property and combining like terms.	I can solve linear equations that have one solution, no solution, or infinitely many solutions. I can use the distributive property and combine like terms to simplify equations. I can solve equations that include fractions and decimals.	Introduce academic vocabulary words in context, not isolation (for example, "Here's the word coefficient in a problem we're solving"). **8.EE.C.7—**Model solving an equation step by step while thinking aloud. **8.EE.C.7—**Demonstrate how to color-code to show inverse operations and simplify each side. **8.EE.C.7—**Use the turn-and-talk method for students to engage in structured partner talk: "What step comes next and why?" **8.EE.C.7—**Show how to solve similar problems with progressive complexity (basic → multistep → with fractions). **8.EE.C.7—**Task students with solving real-life word problems involving money, distance, or age with equations. **8.F.B.4—**Begin with a real-world context (for example, "A plumber charges a $75 base rate plus $40 per hour") and model the process step by step.	Cocreate a concept map of academic vocabulary. **8.EE.C.7—**Use algebra tiles to represent terms. Have students physically group like tiles (for example, 2x + 3x = 5x). **8.EE.C.7—**Scaffold with "term trees" where students circle and label like terms. **8.EE.C.7—**Have students simplify increasingly complex expressions without manipulatives. Ask students to add written justifications (for example, "I combined 2x and 3x because they both have the variable x"). **8.EE.C.7—**Have students draw balanced scales to represent equations. **8.EE.C.7—**Demonstrate solving one-step and two-step equations symbolically. **8.EE.C.7—**Have students use area models or algebra tiles to model expressions like 3(x + 2). **8.EE.C.7—**Have students draw area models or use rectangle diagrams to show distribution. Model using color-coding to show how each term is multiplied. **8.EE.C.7—**Have students solve expressions using symbolic rules. Task students with rewriting expressions without models, such as 4(x − 3) = 4x − 12.	Generate an academic vocabulary jeopardy game. Create a budget builder personal finance simulation. Students choose a job with a fixed hourly wage and create a monthly budget. • Students use equations to calculate income (for example, y = 15x, where x = hours). • Model weekly savings goals using linear functions (graph plus equation). • Ask students to solve equations like "How many hours must I work to afford a $350 gaming system if I save $50 a week?"

Figure 3.6: Grade 8 mathematics essential standards instructional menu.

continued ▶

Standard	Learning Targets	Tier 1 Strategies	Tier 2 Strategies	Extension Strategies
8.F.B.4— Construct a function to model a linear relationship. Construct a function to model a linear relationship between two quantities. Determine the rate of change and initial value from a description, table, or graph.	I can identify the rate of change (slope) and initial value (y-intercept) from a table, graph, or description. I can write and interpret a linear function to represent a real-world relationship. I can explain what the slope and y-intercept mean in context.	**8.F.B.4—**Analyze a scenario with students and co-construct the table, function rule, and graph. **8.F.B.4—**Have students work in pairs, small groups, or independently to create functions from new scenarios using all three representations.	**8.F.B.4—**Provide graphing mats and movable point markers such as plastic chips or stickers. Ask students to use color-coded quadrant charts and point plotting games. Have students plot ordered pairs on paper and describe their location using x and y. **8.F.B.4—**Have students use function machines (physical or drawn) to show inputs and outputs. Ask them to drop number cubes or tokens into a "machine" that applies a rule (+2, ×3, and so on). Have students create and complete structured tables with clear input and output columns. Ask students to translate between rules, tables, and algebraic expressions (for example, $y = 2x + 1$). Have them identify the pattern and write the function. **8.F.B.4—**Have students use connecting cubes to physically build stair-step models of slopes (for example, rise 2, run 1). Task them with graphing slope triangles on coordinate grids. Have students use visual slope charts showing rise and run relationships. Demonstrate calculating slope using the formula $(y_2 - y_1) / (x_2 - x_1)$ before asking students to do so.	Task students with designing a theme park ride using linear planning and problem solving. • Students design a ride with cost components (fixed startup plus cost per foot of track or time spent). • Students use a function like $C(x) = 500 + 120x$ to model the cost of building a ride. • Students graph ride length versus total cost and solve for variables such as maximum length under budget. • Finally, students present their ride plan using visual, numerical, and algebraic evidence.

Source for standard: NGA & CCSSO, 2010b.

<table>
<tr><td colspan="2">Students:
Group Focus:
Intervention Menu Strategy:
Materials and Resources:</td></tr>
<tr><td>"I Do"
Modeling</td><td>• Model using explicit language.
• Use think-alouds and visuals.
• Start with prerequisites and work up to the grade-level skill.</td></tr>
<tr><td>"We Do"
Guided
Practice</td><td>• Determine the appropriate level of scaffolding from the heaviest to the least amount of support.
• Students participate in walking through the process.
• Students use think-alouds to talk through the steps.
• Repeat as necessary.</td></tr>
<tr><td>"You Do"
Independent
Practice</td><td>• Students apply their learning in repeated practice sessions until they are ready to be reassessed at grade level.
• Provide feedback to correct mistakes and misconceptions.
• Repeat as necessary.</td></tr>
<tr><td>Prove It</td><td>• Students complete informal assessments independently to prove mastery of the grade-level skill.
• Students who prove mastery move to the next group. Students who did not re-engage in guided and independent practice.</td></tr>
</table>

Figure 3.7: Tier 2 intervention planner.

Visit ***go.SolutionTree.com/RTIatWork*** *for a free reproducible version of this figure.*

release model into Tier 2 planning, teams can systematically scaffold skills, gradually shifting more responsibility to students while still aligning with grade-level standards and accelerating progress toward proficiency. Teachers may spend the initial sessions focusing on modeling and guided practice to ensure students understand the skill and the expectations. As the intervention progresses, more time is devoted to the independent practice portion, allowing students to apply what they have learned with increasing autonomy while the teacher observes and provides support as needed. The final "prove it" portion functions as a built-in assessment check, giving teachers clear, timely information about student mastery and readiness to move on.

Effective Tier 2 group instruction is grounded in clarity, focus, and responsiveness. The structure is fluid, meaning students move in and out of groups as their needs evolve, ensuring that support is timely and aligned with current learning goals.

As previously mentioned, instruction follows a concise minilesson format using a gradual release model with an *I do, we do, you do* format. However, this model isn't as simple as the teacher models it one time, the teacher and students practice together, then the teacher releases students to perform the task independently. It is a recursive approach that allows for repeated guided practice before students work independently, reinforcing understanding and promoting mastery over time. The teacher models the skill with clarity and precision, ensuring students see and hear exactly what is expected. During the *we do* phase, students actively engage with the teacher and peers to practice the skill with scaffolds in place.

In this model, learning is not a linear process but one that deepens over time through multiple exposures to a concept or skill. The recursive sequence embodies this philosophy by gradually shifting cognitive responsibility from teacher to student across multiple cycles. This repetition helps strengthen retention, accuracy, and transfer of learning. According to Barak Rosenshine's (2012) principles of instruction, effective teaching includes presenting new material in small steps, providing ample practice, and engaging students in guided and independent practice spaced out over time. Recursive learning embodies these principles by returning to the skill multiple times within a short instructional period, enabling students to process, rehearse, and refine their thinking.

Appropriate scaffolding is also essential in Tier 2 groups, but it's important to distinguish between scaffolding and rescuing. Scaffolding provides temporary support to help students access the learning independently. Rescuing, by contrast, doesn't allow students the opportunity to struggle productively and develop perseverance. Effective teachers provide just enough support to guide students toward success while gradually removing those supports as students build confidence and competence.

Additionally, a key feature of successful Tier 2 instruction is reducing teacher talk and increasing student talk and action. The goal is to create space for students to verbalize their thinking, make connections, and engage in meaningful practice. Teachers use precise academic language and ensure that the task is explicitly stated so there is no ambiguity in what students are expected to do.

In a high-quality Tier 2 intervention, teachers should dedicate most of the instructional time to structured independent practice where students actively engage with the targeted skill. This focused practice is essential for developing mastery, as it allows students to apply what they have learned while receiving timely, specific feedback from the teacher. Repeated and deliberate practice strengthens neural pathways, increasing the likelihood of accurate retrieval and application of the skill during assessments or in new contexts. Prioritizing student practice not only reinforces learning but also builds confidence and promotes long-term retention.

Intervention Scenario

In this section, we present a real-world Tier 2 instruction scenario, illustrating how educators can design, implement, and adjust interventions in ELA. This scenario provides concrete examples of tailoring instruction to target specific skill gaps, incorporate hands-on and scaffolded strategies, and respond to ongoing student data. It highlights practical decision-making processes, from selecting appropriate materials and grouping students to monitoring progress and modifying instruction as needed. By examining this example, you can see how Tier 2 interventions function in practice, building both teacher confidence and student success.

After reviewing the latest common assessment with her English I team, Ms. Brown and her colleagues noticed a pattern: Several students struggled with a key standard, RL.9-10.3 (NGA & CCSSO, 2010a), which focuses on analyzing how complex characters with conflicting motivations impact a story's events. While most of their students demonstrated proficiency, twelve students across the team's classes consistently missed the mark when it came to identifying internal character conflict and explaining how it drives the plot forward.

Each student's classroom teacher has already held feedback conversations with them about the assessment results. Through these conversations, students received clarity on what they specifically need to improve and how they can demonstrate their understanding with evidence from the text. This preparation ensures that the intervention time is focused, intentional, and aligned to the learning target.

Recognizing this gap, Ms. Brown plans a targeted small-group intervention to provide these students with the additional support they need. The following scenario illustrates how she uses intentional scaffolding, modeling, and guided practice to help students meet the learning target and grow toward proficiency, beginning with the intervention planner shown in figure 3.8.

Students: *Aaliyah, Amir, Fatima, Diego, Chloe, Isaiah, Maya, Elijah, Nia, Kai, Sofia, Juan*

Group Focus: *Students should be able to analyze how a character's conflicting motivations impact their actions and how that develops the plot. Students need additional support identifying and analyzing conflicting character motivations and how they impact the development of the plot.*

Intervention Menu Strategy: *In addition to a think-aloud, students will use a visual organizer in the form of a Motivation, Action, Plot chart as a scaffold to track characters' internal conflicts and their influence on story events.*

Figure 3.8: Tier 2 intervention planner for Ms. Brown's ELA class.

continued ▶

<table>
<tr><td colspan="2">Materials and Resources:
Short scene from Romeo and Juliet, act 3, scene 1; last chapter of Of Mice and Men; excerpt from The Hate U Give; clip from Hair Love
Motivation, Action, Plot chart (graphic organizer)
Whiteboard or chart paper
Highlighters and pencils
Sticky notes for exit slip</td></tr>
<tr><td>"I Do"
Modeling</td><td>• Model the think-aloud.
• Model identifying conflicting motivations and their impact on the plot by revisiting a familiar excerpt from Romeo and Juliet.</td></tr>
<tr><td>"We Do"
Guided
Practice</td><td>• Complete an example together using the last chapter from Of Mice and Men.
• Students write example in graphic organizer.</td></tr>
<tr><td>"You Do"
Independent
Practice</td><td>• Read an excerpt from The Hate U Give.
• Students record conflicting motivations, character actions, and the impact on the plot.</td></tr>
<tr><td>Prove It</td><td>• Watch a video clip of Hair Love.
• Students complete an exit slip summarizing conflicting motivations, character actions, and the impact on the plot.</td></tr>
</table>

Figure 3.9 is an example of the exit slip referred to in the planner in figure 3.8.

Name: ______________________________

Date: ______________________________

Watch the video clip from *Hair Love*.

Write a brief response that explains the conflicting motivations of the character, the actions the character took, and the impact on the overall plot.

____

____

____

____

____

Figure 3.9: Exit slip.

During her Tier 2 intervention session, Ms. Brown projects an excerpt from *Romeo and Juliet.*

Ms. Brown: Today we're going to focus on conflicting motivations, when a character wants two things at once and those things don't go together. That inner tug-of-war is what makes characters feel real and makes the plot move. Let's start with Romeo.

She reads aloud the quote.

"O, I am fortune's fool!"

Ms. Brown (thinking aloud): Hmm... Romeo just killed Tybalt, but listen to what he says here. "I am fortune's fool." That tells me he regrets what just happened. Why would he feel that way? What were his motivations?

Isaiah: He was trying to defend Mercutio.

Fatima: But he also just married Juliet. Tybalt is her cousin.

Ms. Brown: Exactly. So, he's stuck. On one side, he wants revenge for his friend. On the other, he wants peace because of his love for Juliet. That's a conflict. Let's write that down.

Ms. Brown models writing the conflicting motivations in the graphic organizer.

Ms. Brown: So, what action does Romeo take because of these motivations?

Diego: He kills Tybalt.

Ms. Brown: Right. And what does that do to the plot?

Chloe: It made the fight worse, like he had to leave Verona.

Ms. Brown: Exactly. One decision, caused by two opposite motivations, pushes the entire story forward. That's what we mean when we say character motivations impact the plot.

Ms. Brown hands out a shorter excerpt from *Of Mice and Men*, near the ending.

Ms. Brown: Let's try one together now. Read this part where George is talking to Lennie near the river. Think about what George wants and how that affects his decision.

Students silently read the paragraph as Ms. Brown scaffolds the reading as necessary.

Ms. Brown: Partner up. Work with your partner to find what George's two motivations are here. What's the conflict inside him?

Students share their responses.

Maya: He wants to protect Lennie, and he also knows the other guys will hurt him worse.

Ms. Brown: Yes. George wants to be kind, but he also feels responsible. What does he do because of that conflict?

Amir: Lennie shoots himself.

Ms. Brown: And how does that affect the plot?

Nia: It ends their dream. Everything they were working toward is gone.

Ms. Brown: Perfect. That's how we break down internal conflict and see its ripple effects in the story. Up next, you'll get to try this yourselves using the text *The Hate U Give*. You will use the same organizer to record conflicting motivations, character actions, and the impact on the plot. When I begin seeing you are able to identify these on your own, I will give you an exit slip to show me evidence that you can recognize the conflicting motivations and the impact on the plot this week. Remember, this organizer to help you clearly express your ideas. If you can show me evidence of mastery, we can mark it in your goal books and move you on to your next goal.

In this scenario, Ms. Brown models how to identify conflicting character motivations and see how they affect the plot, using a graphic organizer to make her thinking clear. She gradually shifts responsibility to the students, first guiding discussion with events from *Romeo and Juliet* and then supporting partner work with *Of Mice and Men*. Students practice finding internal conflicts, predicting character actions, and connecting those actions to the story. In Tier 2 interventions, it is important to recognize that students may need multiple "you do" intervention sessions before they are ready for the "prove it" assessment. This extended practice allows learners to develop the automaticity and confidence required to apply the skill independently. With scaffolding, guided practice, and chances to work independently, students build their skills while the teacher checks understanding, gives feedback, and sets clear goals. This approach helps students understand character motivations and their impact on the plot in a clear, structured way.

Are You Ready?

Tier 2 instruction plays a critical role in ensuring that all students have the opportunity to learn at high levels, both at grade level and beyond. It is not merely a support for struggling learners but a strategic approach to address individual needs, accelerate growth, and close learning gaps through focused, skill-specific instruction.

To help students reach their full academic potential, educators must commit to intentionally embedding time within the school day for targeted intervention and meaningful extension. This commitment reflects a belief in equity, ensuring every learner receives the instruction, support, and challenge they need to succeed.

Achieving this level of instructional precision requires teacher teams to develop a clear understanding of the distinctions between Tier 1 and Tier 2 instruction. While Tier 1 provides a strong foundation for all students, Tier 2 demands a shift in mindset and practice, moving from whole-group reteaching to responsive, data-informed, small-group instruction.

Developing well-structured instructional menus and lesson planning frameworks is essential in this process. These tools streamline planning, clarify instructional goals, and reduce guesswork when responding to student needs. By proactively outlining strategies for intervention and extension, teams can ensure that instruction is purposeful, aligned to standards, and adaptable to diverse learners.

When schools prioritize Tier 2 planning as an integral part of their instructional systems, the result is a more cohesive, consistent, and effective approach to student support. This intentional design empowers educators to meet students where they are and guide them forward with confidence, ensuring that no student is left behind and every student is given the chance to excel.

To become more effective in planning intentional Tier 2 intervention, the teacher team reflects on both the strengths and areas for refinement in the planning and delivery of Tier 2 intervention. This reflection helps identify potential barriers, whether in logistics or in the instructional design itself, so teachers can adjust with intention. Yet even the strongest plan is only part of the equation. For intervention to truly have impact, students must see value in the work, believe growth is possible, and take an active role in their progress. Sustained success depends not only on what teachers plan and deliver, but also on how students engage with it and begin to take ownership of their learning journey. The guiding coalition also solicits this feedback to determine what is working in the Tier 2 intervention system, what systemwide changes teachers may need to make, or what professional learning teachers need to grow their expertise to provide highly effective instruction. After your team has assessed your readiness, use the reflection questions in the reproducible tool "Pause and Take Action: Chapter 3" to determine the next steps to build your Tier 2 intervention system.

Pause and Take Action: Chapter 3

Consider the following questions to determine your teacher team's next instruction design actions.

- How does our team plan Tier 1 and Tier 2 strategies for teaching, intervening, and extending the learning? Do we plan intentionally? How could menus and planning documents like the I do, we do, you do model strengthen the instruction in Tier 2 intervention?
- Are our intervention strategies focused, hands on, and taught with the appropriate level of scaffolding?
- Do our extension activities promote higher-order thinking skills and application? Do students have opportunities to choose an extension or help design their own extension?
- Does our team have a planning structure or document for small-group instruction that aligns with the recursive learning model (I do, we do, you do)?
- Are our students clear that when they engage in their intervention and extension time, it is to work on a specific essential standard or learning goal and not just because their overall score was low (or high if in extension)?
- Does our intervention include a progress-monitoring component that allows for flexible groupings? Once students show mastery, are they able to flexibly move to a group that continues to guide their growth and achievement?

Team Action Steps

Now that you've reflected, identify two strengths in your teacher team practice related to intervention and extension.

Identify two next steps your team will take to deepen their Tier 2 intervention work and when those steps will occur.

Second Helpings © 2027 Solution Tree Press • SolutionTree.com
Visit **go.SolutionTree.com/RTIatWork** to download this free reproducible.

CHAPTER 4

Fostering Student Ownership

When inviting guests to dinner, the host clearly outlines the details of the evening, including what is on the menu, when and where it will take place, and any other details to ensure the guests have clear expectations. Some of the most beautiful, meaningful, long-lasting, and memorable meals are when all those attending provide insight into what they like, need, or need to avoid and contribute to the time together by bringing something to add to the meal. Often, the host will ask guests what they like, their allergies, or even what they need in terms of the space to enjoy the time together. Some may be allergic to or afraid of pets. Other guests may not be able to climb stairs or walk on uneven ground. The food, location, and setup of a meal together is better when the host understands the strengths, likes, and limitations of the guests. More information about who the guests are allows for a meaningful and successful meal. In the same way, teacher teams create clarity around the essential learning and share it intentionally so students know the goals and direction. Teams continue to foster this investment as they check in with their "guests" about how they're doing and what they need to be successful.

The second part of this partnership or ownership in the time together is cocreating the meal. This sense of communicating clearly and then listening and gathering feedback builds trust. When guests contribute something to the meal, they are part of the design, and when people are part of the creation of something, they invest in the experience and outcome. This is the center of student ownership—listening to build trust and cocreating or contributing to build investment and ownership.

Finally, the host encourages guests to engage and be themselves at the dinner party, leaning into their strengths or who they are. Some love to tell stories, others love to ask questions, maybe others sit quietly taking it all in and will engage later on as they feel comfortable. The host invites guests into the conversation, aware of how each is feeling, engaging, or withdrawing. Teacher teams, in a similar fashion, ask students to consider where they are in their learning and build confidence in taking action to deepen their learning. When we approach Tier 2 intervention systems with a sense of clarity and build a culture of trust and ownership, more students will achieve at high levels.

Teacher teams systematically and collaboratively respond to students who need additional time to learn grade-level essentials. This response is most powerful when students reflect on what helps them learn and what gets in the way. As students learn about their own patterns of thinking, they not only begin to achieve but also build confidence that will transfer to multiple situations and learning.

This chapter describes the purpose and research base for student investment and provides actions teacher teams can take that lead to student investment. While the focus of this book is Tier 2 intervention, these actions also apply to Tier 1 instruction. These actions are rooted in three questions that students must answer throughout the learning process: "Where am I going?", "Where am I now?", and "How do I close the gap?" But first, let's explore why student investment is so important.

The Purpose of Fostering Student Ownership

Teachers are only part of the equation when it comes to building effective and sustainable Tier 2 intervention systems. For these systems to have lasting impact and truly accelerate learning, students must be invested in the process. That investment starts with students believing that their time spent in intervention is meaningful, that the support they're receiving is purposeful, and that they are capable of mastering essential learning.

Many students who require additional time and support have faced repeated challenges in the past. Their confidence may be fragile. Their self-talk may include statements like, "I'm just not good at this," or "I always need extra help," or worse, "I'll never get it." Without intentional shifts in how intervention is communicated and experienced, these mindsets can persist and quietly undermine even the most well-designed instructional efforts.

Before anything else, students receiving Tier 2 intervention must believe one key understanding: Intervention is not a punishment.

Too often, learners internalize the message that needing help is a form of failure. When intervention feels like a consequence—missing out on a preferred activity, being pulled from class, or being singled out—it can reinforce the very narratives educators want to rewrite. To change this, teachers must reframe intervention as a signal that they believe in their students' potential. Teachers must convey that all students matter and that they know, with a little more time and support, students receiving Tier 2 interventions can and will learn at high levels.

When students understand the purpose of intervention, when they see it as personalized time for growth rather than remediation or repetition, they start to show up differently. They participate more willingly. They take risks. They begin to expect growth. They persist until they achieve. The role of the teacher team in building this sense of ownership occurs in how the team designs assessments, facilitates instruction and intervention, and notices the impact of assessment design, instruction, and intervention on students' achievement and confidence. Based on how students are responding and what they are experiencing, teachers adjust to ensure students learn more and gain confidence.

Student efficacy is central to student investment, as research shows that when individuals believe their actions lead to growth and improvement, they are more engaged and persistent (Bandura, 1997). Student investment strategies lead to students believing that if they engage in instruction or intervention, then they will learn the essential standards. When they believe and have efficacy, they will persist longer, which leads to higher achievement (Marques, Gallagher, & Lopez, 2017; Marques, Lopez, & Mitchell, 2013).

Students need to believe that if they engage in the intervention, then it is actually going to help them; the more they believe this, the more they will build efficacy and persist in learning. Similarly, teacher efficacy matters, since the more teachers believe that their actions help students achieve the essential standards, the more confidently and attentively they will design Tier 2 interventions. Hattie (2023) synthesizes decades of research and emphasizes that teacher efficacy is not simply confidence but a combination of mind frames, intentional alignment of learning intentions, success criteria, assessments, strategies, and ongoing evaluative thinking about impact. Effective teachers consistently ask whether their teaching led to the intended learning and what evidence supports that, yet many plateau after their early years because they do not fully adopt reflective, learning-oriented mind frames (Hattie, 2023).

Research identifies collective teacher efficacy as among the most powerful influences on student learning (Goddard et al., 2000; Hattie, 2023). *Collective teacher efficacy* refers to the shared belief among educators that together they can influence student outcomes. When teachers work collaboratively and view themselves as agents of change, their collective impact is magnified (Hattie, 2023). Teacher teams continue to develop efficacy as they analyze assessment evidence, plan interventions for collective implementation, and include each student's ability to partner in the intervention.

Teacher mindset and language matter. When educators consistently and sincerely express confidence in students' abilities, students internalize those beliefs. When teachers say, "I'm pulling you into this group because I know you can do it," it changes the narrative. It signals intentionality to students when teachers design interventions that are targeted, time bound, and tailored to student needs. When those interventions are accompanied by clear explanations, celebrations of growth, and opportunities for student agency, they become more than support; they become empowerment.

The goal isn't just to help students catch up—it's to help them *improve and develop confidence to own their learning*. When they have the tools to understand their learning, reflect on their progress, and take ownership of their growth, students move from simply being compliant and completing "enough work" to developing commitment and confidence in learning the essential standards, articulating what that standard is, and knowing they have learned it.

Tier 2 interventions are most successful when students feel seen, supported, and capable. When they know where they're going, where they are now, and how to close the gap, they don't just invest in intervention; they invest in themselves. Tier 2 can't simply be a program or place where students go to get more help. It must be a process that intentionally includes students as powerful partners in ensuring learning at high levels.

Further, this concept of efficacy and belief plays out in a specific set of actions that lead to students being able to address their own learning strengths and needs. One powerful research-based framework for building student investment is rooted in the following three core questions, originally framed by D. Royce Sadler (1989).

1. **Where am I going?** Students know and understand the learning they are working to achieve. When asked about their work during class, students respond with comments about what they are learning versus what they are doing. Teacher teams facilitate the design of the assessment to help students connect their learning to the assessment evidence. Teachers share learning targets and standards with students

and guide instructional activities to help them understand what qualities must appear in their work to achieve the learning target and standards. Instructional interventions help and guide students to further understand the qualities and the learning parts they need to achieve that lead to being proficient on the entire standard. Interventions help students see examples of both high-quality and lesser-quality work so they can see the difference. Teacher clarity is one of the highest leverage actions that leads to learning and student clarity (Goodwin & Rouleau, 2022; Hattie, 2023).

2. **Where am I now?** Students can articulate their strengths and next steps in terms of their learning the essential standards. This self-assessment process is critical to students investing in their learning and taking ownership of engaging deeply with teachers as they learn more, particularly when it gets tough. Ensuring students understand their strengths is a key piece in developing confidence and perseverance (Andrade et al., 2019; Andrade & Brookhart, 2020; Duckworth, 2016; Hattie, 2023). To that end, teacher teams facilitate and embrace a practice of self-assessment so students can reflect on where they are. This also includes students tracking their progress and reflecting on what is helping them grow and learn. This process is central to students learning how to learn (Andrade et al., 2019). For all students, and especially for students who need more time, this approach to helping them understand what works for them is essential to sustainable success.
3. **How do I close the gap?** As students learn where they are in terms of their strengths and next steps and can reflect on what helps or hinders their learning, they are able to take action. Some of this action will be facilitated as a team approach in Tier 2 intervention, so guiding students in the intervention and helping them develop the ability to name what they need to achieve the essential standards is part of the ownership process. The design of the assessment, the student tracking tools, and the facilitation of the intervention are also framed within learning and lead to ownership and transferable skills. It is the action and the moment students recognize that it is working that make efficacy take hold.

In summary, student investment is a partnership between student and teacher, and good instructional practices lead to a culture where students learn how to learn and take steps to grow with greater independence. We will use these core questions as a framework for the next section, when we explore student investment in action.

Heidi L. Andrade and Susan M. Brookhart (2020) argue that classroom assessment should be understood as a process of *coregulation of learning*, where teachers and students work together to guide progress toward goals. They emphasize that assessment is not just about measuring learning but also about actively shaping it through feedback, self-assessment, and peer interactions. Andrade and Brookhart (2020) describe coregulation as involving three interconnected processes.

1. **Teacher regulation:** Teachers design learning intentions, success criteria, and assessment tasks that make expectations clear.
2. **Self-regulation:** Students monitor their own progress, use feedback, and develop agency in their learning.
3. **Coregulation:** Teachers and peers provide guidance, scaffolding, and dialogue that help students engage in productive self-regulation.

Andrade and Brookhart (2020) highlight the importance of formative assessment practices—such as goal setting, feedback, and revision—as tools that move students from dependence on teacher direction toward greater autonomy. Effective assessment, in this model, balances teacher support with opportunities for students to take responsibility for their own learning. Ultimately, Andrade and Brookhart (2020) position classroom assessment as a shared responsibility between teachers and students, designed to build students' capacity to regulate their learning, develop confidence, and achieve at higher levels.

We've included specific strategies for Tier 2 interventions in the following sections. You might also choose to use some of these strategies in your Tier 1 instruction.

Student Ownership in Action

Student investment plays out in real time before, during, and after the unit instruction. Each of the three questions from the preceding section has potential concrete actions, as detailed in the following sections, that teacher teams can take to ensure learning. While it is possible to use these strategies at different times, it is important to ensure students have answers to each question, since they build on one another.

Where Am I Going?

To answer this question, students need clarity on the learning targets. They need to know exactly what success looks like, not just for the unit or the test, but for the essential skills that will serve them long after the intervention ends. Teachers can make this visible by taking the following actions.

- Share "I can" statements in student-friendly language in instruction and to start intervention, placing those learning targets right on the assessment itself.
- Break down complex standards into understandable learning goals or targets and put them in order from simple to complex. Include examples of each learning target alongside the standards. This is often the student-friendly version of the learning progression or proficiency scale.
- Use exemplars, rubrics, and models to illustrate what proficiency looks like. These can facilitate conversations with students so they start to embrace the learning language of the standard. Use these as graphic organizers for students to work through with a partner.
- Use examples that show possible mistakes and misconceptions and then more quality responses so students have a clear distinction between where they are and where they need to go.

When students understand the destination, they are more likely to stay engaged in the journey.

Where Am I Now?

Honest, nonjudgmental feedback helps students see their current level of understanding. This isn't about scores, it's about information. Assessment data, quick checks, and reflective conversations give students insight into their current progress. This insight needs to include strengths as well as next steps to grow. Strategies include the following.

- Provide annotated work samples with clear feedback. Share strengths before next steps.
- Model how to apply the feedback and then have students practice revising examples using the feedback. Students often don't know how to interpret feedback, especially students who are the beginning of understanding.
- Facilitate self-assessment using rubrics or checklists. It is important to model self-assessment as some students need guidance to reflect and talk about the qualities of learning rather than just determine whether something is right or wrong. Specifically, have students self-evaluate the errors made on the end-of-unit assessment or any assessment that led to additional time and support in intervention.

- Use visuals (such as progress bars or goal trackers) to show growth over time.

When students see that they are making progress, even in small steps, they begin to build momentum and trust the process.

How Do I Close the Gap?

This is where student investment begins to be transferable and sustainable. When learners know what to do next and believe and see that effort leads to improvement, they are more likely to persist. Effective strategies to foster this belief include the following.

- Collaboratively set short-term, achievable goals on the essential standards. Engage in targeted reflection on which actions led to progress and goal achievement and which actions or inactions led to not achieving the goal. This helps students learn and make connections on their patterns of work and learning. Goal setting also helps students celebrate the small wins along the way, which is essential for developing persistence and momentum.
- Give students voice and choice in how they practice or demonstrate learning. Once teacher teams have set the essential standards, along with the criteria that describe which qualities demonstrate proficiency, they can create choices that align to those essential standards. Students can then choose which activity or task they will engage in to learn more or even to show their learning. The qualities or criteria of the essential standard are the same, but the task, work, or activity may vary.
- Build in regular reflection by asking the following questions: What strategy worked? What will I try next? When did I get stuck? What did I do when I got stuck? What was confusing? When I got confused, what did I do? What questions do I have about this task or this learning? How does this learning connect to other important things?

Students must not only be able to answer the question "What am I doing?" but also be able to answer "Why am I doing it?" Being able to connect an intervention task to a specific skill they're building transforms that task into a stepping-stone to sustainable and transferable learning.

One tool to achieve this is a student goal-tracking book. This strategy guides students to invest in and address those three questions. This powerful tool visually tracks and celebrates student learning across both academic skills and essential dispositions. Structured as a personal portfolio or journal, the goal tracker includes clear, student-friendly "I can" statements aligned with key learning targets. As students demonstrate mastery, whether it's decoding words, showing determination, or applying a growth mindset, they earn recognition that is documented in their book. This recognition represents tangible milestones in their learning journey and connects the evidence of learning and assessment to their growth and achievement. It also helps teacher teams focus on what matters most not only in their Tier 1 instruction but also in Tier 2 intervention. If students aren't achieving the essentials, the student goal-tracking book can bridge instruction in Tier 1 with instruction and intervention in Tier 2 for both students and teachers.

The goal-tracker model in figure 4.1 (page 90) is a powerful visual and instructional tool that not only communicates academic expectations but also cultivates key learning dispositions. This structure is adaptable to multiple grade levels and courses. Additionally, a goal tracker provides a student-friendly version of the proficiency scales and learning progressions teachers use to plan Tier 1 and 2 instruction. This allows transparency for students and serves as a visual reminder of their grade-level expectations. The example in figure 4.1 has the goal of *decoding*, is designed for first-grade learners, and integrates application (level 3.0), knowledge (level 2.0), and insight (level 1.0) to promote student agency and mastery. In this section, we explore how the structure, language, and intent of this decoding goal tracker develop positive student dispositions while supporting core academic standards.

The decoding goal tracker is organized into the following four domains. Each of these domains supports a different cognitive and dispositional focus, creating a layered framework that encourages students to understand what they are learning, why it matters, and how they can demonstrate mastery.

- **Application (level 3.0)** specifies the grade-level expectation of real-world reading outcomes students can achieve.
- **Knowledge (level 2.0)** lists prerequisite skills such as key vocabulary, conceptual understanding, and learning targets related to decoding.
- **Insight (level 1.0)** encourages awareness of readiness or foundational skills with assistance.
- **Transfer (level 4.0)** extends the broader purpose, using strategies to figure out unknown words.

This scaffolded design is more than instructional; it is dispositional. It shows students how their growing knowledge connects to practical use and how they can take ownership of the learning process. While this example shows what this

Decoding

Application (level 3)

- I can read two syllable words like *sunset* and *basket*.
- I can read long vowel pattern words like *cake*, *boat*, *team*, and *glue*.
- I can read words with affixes like *jumped* and *running*.

Knowledge (level 2)

Key vocabulary: *base word*, *blend*, *consonant*, *decode*, *digraph*, *silent e*, *suffix*, *vowel*

- I can identify the sounds *-ed*, *-ing*, *-s*, and *-es* make.
- I can identify the sounds *-ai*, *-ay*,*-ea*, *-ey*, *-ee*, *-oo*, *-ue*, *-ie*, *-oa*, and *-ow* make.
- I can break words into syllables or parts.
- I can read words like *flag*, *ship*, and *dish*.
- I can read words like *cat*, *mop*, and *sit*.

Insight (level 1)

- I can name letters and say the sounds.
- I can blend sounds to make words.

Transfer (level 4)

I can use what I know about sound patterns to read longer, trickier words like *lightning* and *replacing*.

First-Grade Mastery Standard: RF.1.3

Source for standard: NGA & CCSSO, 2010a.

Source: © 2024 by Autumn Mosby and Josh Depoe. Used with permission.

Figure 4.1: Grade 1 goal-tracker example.

model looks like in first grade, it is adaptable across grade level and course with minor adjustments. The main idea is that students document their progress as they achieve each essential standard.

Let's take a closer look at each of these learning-progression levels in the tracker. As we dive deeper into each section, you will see how these academic skills also connect with key learning dispositions, which are often a barrier for students. In Tier 2, teaching students to believe they can achieve high levels of learning is equally important as the interventions and extensions themselves. Chapter 5 will provide a more in-depth look at these dispositions and their impact on learning.

Application: Fostering Independence and Goal Setting

At the heart of the decoding goal tracker is the application (3.0) section, where students see the grade-level requirements to achieve grade-level proficiency. These empowering "I can" statements set the tone of capability and ownership. Students are invited to demonstrate their mastery by checking off three specific targets, such as the following.

1. I can read long vowel pattern words like *bake*, *team*, *boat*, and *glue*.
2. I can read two-syllable words like *sunset* or *basket*.
3. I can read words with affixes like *jumped* and *running*.

These specific skills are not only imperative to developing reading fluency, but are also bite sized and measurable, allowing students to self-monitor and celebrate progress. The checkbox format offers a visual representation of growth, which fosters motivation and goal setting. Chapter 5 provides more information on learning dispositions (including the following).

- **Independence:** Students learn that reading is something they can do on their own through practice.
- **Goal orientation:** The checklist format prompts students to work toward completing a challenge.
- **Perseverance:** Students are likely to encounter struggle (such as decoding multisyllabic words and long vowel pattern words), and the clear objectives give them reason to keep trying.

As students consistently show mastery in application, teachers often celebrate student success by awarding physical badges, stickers, stamps, and classroom recognition among peers, reinforcing that academic achievement is both personal and social.

Knowledge: Building Conceptual Understanding and Language Precision

The knowledge (2.0) section focuses on key decoding vocabulary: *base word*, *blend*, *consonant*, *decode*, *digraph*, *silent e*, *suffix*, and *vowel*. This vocabulary is not just a list of terms; it represents a reminder of the importance of using relevant academic language. Students are being introduced to the language of readers, and when they use terms like *vowel* or *silent e* in their reading and writing discussions, they are stepping into the role of expert learner. Mastering these terms fosters academic self-concept; using precise language helps students feel like capable members of a scholarly community. When students possess the vocabulary to describe their reading strategies, they are more likely to reflect on their successes and challenges, ask for help in specific ways, and internalize the logic of the English language.

In addition to key vocabulary, a series of student-friendly "I can" statements like the following outline the core decoding behaviors.

- I can identify the sounds *-ed*, *-ing*, *-s*, and *-es* make.
- I can identify the sounds *-ai*, *-ay*, *-ea*, *-ey*, *-ee*, *-oo*, *-ue*, *-ie*, *-oa*, and *-ow* make.
- I can break words into syllables or parts.
- I can read words like *flag*, *ship*, and *dish*.
- I can read words like *cat*, *mop*, and *sit*.

These "I can" statements serve a dual purpose. First, they describe the progressive skills necessary to become a fluent decoder; second, they promote a mindset of agency. Rather than being told what to do, students are invited to take responsibility for their learning. These statements foster the following dispositions.

- **Self-efficacy:** Students believe they can learn and apply new strategies.
- **Metacognition:** By naming the parts of words and sounds, students begin to think about their thinking and reading processes.
- **Cognitive flexibility:** Understanding that letters can behave differently depending on context (for example, silent e) encourages mental adaptability.
- **Ownership of learning:** Framing skills as "I can" statements puts the learner at the center.
- **Task commitment:** Students begin to understand the step-by-step nature of mastering complex reading behaviors.

Students track their ability to use these skills during independent practice and Tier 2 group instruction. Teachers can also use the statements to guide their conversations and provide specific feedback to the learner.

Insight: Supporting Guided Reflection

The insight (1.0) section focuses on the prerequisite skills or simpler skills and processes required to succeed throughout the learning progression. In the area of decoding, these simpler processes display the following "I can" statements.

- I can name letters and say the sounds.
- I can blend sounds to make words.

These statements might appear simple, but they are key foundational skills that will accelerate students' growth toward grade-level proficiency, as well as convey profound dispositional power. First graders are just beginning to understand that growth takes time, effort, and support. Feeling some instant success within these simpler processes motivates them to continue to grow and progress toward grade-level mastery. This encourages the following dispositions.

- **Growth mindset:** Students understand that ability grows with effort and support.
- **Help-seeking behavior:** Normalizing help fosters a culture where students are more willing to ask questions or accept guidance.
- **Resilience:** By recognizing that practice is part of learning, students develop patience and endurance.

Teachers can use "I can" statements to initiate learning conferences, set growth goals, or reflect with students on how support contributed to their success.

Transfer: Thinking Strategically Beyond the Lesson

The last critical piece of the tracker is the extended learning outcome, transfer (4.0). The statement that represents this level is "I can use what I know about sound patterns to read longer words like *lightning* or *replacing*."

Transfer represents the highest cognitive demand of the decoding goal. It moves students beyond grade-level skills into real-time strategy use, requiring flexible application in unfamiliar contexts. This transfer outcome builds the following dispositions.

- **Strategic thinking:** Students learn to select and apply appropriate decoding tools when encountering a challenge.
- **Self-regulation:** Transfer requires pausing, analyzing, and adjusting, which are all core behaviors of metacognitive learners.

- **Confidence in uncertainty:** By embracing the unknown word as an opportunity, students shift from avoidance to curiosity.

Teachers who emphasize transfer help students see that the purpose of decoding is not to complete worksheets or pass isolated reading assessments, but to unlock meaning and comprehension across various types of texts. That vision connects academic skill to lifelong learning dispositions.

When students see themselves as capable, strategic readers, they carry that belief into every domain of learning. And it starts with clear, visible goals and a community of support that believes every learner can grow.

Student Goal-Tracking Scenarios

The following scenario illustrates how Mrs. Corl, a middle school mathematics teacher, created goal-tracking posters for her classroom to help students take ownership of their learning. She believes every student deserves to know the essential skills they're expected to master by the end of eighth grade.

> **Mrs. Corl:** All right everyone, before I begin today's lesson, I want to draw your attention to the goal-tracking posters for our new unit about functions. We have two essential standards that we will be tracking progress toward throughout the unit. Let's look at each one so that you know what evidence you will need to provide me to show you are becoming proficient.

Mrs. Corl directs her students' attention to the goal tracker posters hanging on the wall displaying the following two standards and the learning targets.

- **Application (3.0): 8.F.A.2**—Compare properties of two functions each represented in a different way.
  - Compare characteristics of two functions represented in different ways.
  - Compare slopes of two functions represented in different ways.
  - Compare the y-intercepts of two functions in different ways.
- **Application (3.0): 8.F.B.5**—Describe the functional relationship between two quantities by analyzing a graph.
  - Describe the qualitative relationship between two quantities by analyzing a graph.
  - Explain how one quantity changes as the other increases or decreases.
  - Describe key patterns in the graph such as increasing, decreasing, or constant sections.

Mrs. Corl reads the learning targets from the application (3.0) section of the tracker poster for both standards, front-loading key academic vocabulary students will hear in the upcoming unit. As Mrs. Corl reads, a student responds.

> ***Damon:*** Sounds hard. I don't understand what any of that means.
>
> ***Mrs. Corl:*** That's OK. It might sound hard right now, but when we begin to get into the lessons, it will get easier. As a reminder, though, what are some ways you can deal with the frustrations of learning something new?
>
> ***Laney:*** You always tell us to ask questions the moment it gets tricky and to be OK if something isn't easy the first time.
>
> ***Mrs. Corl:*** Right! Make sure you speak up and not give up. Each week in our unit, I will give a short quiz to check your progress toward these goals. As you show me evidence of your progress, we will celebrate meeting your goals, and you can sign the poster. As always, if I see students needing more practice, I will provide specific bell work at the beginning of class that focuses on those areas where you might be struggling.

Throughout the unit, Mrs. Corl uses assessments and the tracking sheets to give students personalized feedback based on ongoing data. Students are encouraged to reflect on their progress, identify areas for growth, and celebrate their successes. When they demonstrate mastery of the level 3 goals, they get to sign their name on a classroom poster, making their achievement visible and meaningful. The bell work Mrs. Corl referred to takes the form of short, specific, targeted practice sheets that tailor previously taught concepts to students' specific needs that they complete at the start of every class period. With these strategies. Mrs. Corl embeds intentional intervention throughout the unit.

Because Mrs. Corl has built a positive and collaborative classroom culture, students genuinely cheer each other on. Everyone participates in celebrating growth. Goal tracking turns into more than just a tool; it becomes a shared experience that motivates and empowers all learners.

In the next scenario, Ms. Robbins, a grade 2 teacher, also believes that all her second graders are capable of taking charge of their own learning. Every student in the preK through grade 4 building has a goal-tracking portfolio that outlines all the essential standards they're expected to master by the end of their grade level.

Each day, Ms. Robbins dedicates thirty minutes to one hour of instructional time for students to work on a self-selected goal. She's set up a goal workstation in the classroom with drawers labeled by goal so students can easily find the materials they need. While students are engaged in their independent practice, Ms. Robbins uses part of that time to work with small Tier 2 groups, providing targeted support based on the specific learning targets students need more help with, identified through her ongoing data analysis.

Ms. Robbins: OK class, just a reminder, this is your time to work on practicing the goals you haven't mastered yet. I filled our drawers with new activities for you to choose from. Remember, I may be working with a group of students, so if you finish, sign your name on the board to show me you are ready to confer with me about your completed activity. I will check it, and we will mark your progress in your tracker together.

Ms. Robbins pulls a group to her table, asking students to bring their goal tracker with them.

Ms. Robbins: OK, everyone, the last assessment we took on text features showed me that you need a little more practice and support. Let's look at what you did well first. All of you did a great job using the table of contents and headings to answer questions, so let's check those learning targets in your tracker. Where we need a little more practice is using visuals like diagrams and photographs to answer questions. That's what we are going to practice together today.

Ms. Robbins engages students in a lesson about using visual information. She employs modeling and guided practice of specific strategies to support the students in the group.

Ms. Robbins: Now it is your turn to practice on your own. This text is about butterfly life cycles. Make sure to use the visuals in the text to help you answer the questions. Take this activity back to your seat to work. When you finish, make sure to sign the board to let me know you are ready to confer with me and maybe even earn your stamp of proficiency for this standard!

As Ms. Robbins releases students, she notices Bryan is not starting on the task. Ms. Robbins walks over to him to investigate.

Ms. Robbins: Hey, what's going on? Do you have a question?

Bryan: This is too hard. I can't do it.

Ms. Robbins: I know that can feel frustrating, but remember what we say in this classroom? We can do hard things. Not everything will come easy the first time, but when we keep practicing, we learn new things. Focus on practicing the strategy we did together at the table, taking it one step at a time. What's the first thing you need to do?

Bryan: I need to read the text and pay attention to the diagram.

Ms. Robbins: You got it! Do that first, then try answering the questions. I will check in with you again when you are done, and we will discuss your progress.

Ms. Robbins also sets aside the last fifteen minutes of the hour to hold one-on-one conferences. During the conference, students bring their work, and Ms. Robbins compares it to the related goal page in their tracker. Together, they review the evidence, talk through what's going well, and identify next steps. If the student has met the standard, they add that work to their portfolio as proof of mastery and receive a stamp in their tracker.

To wrap up class, Ms. Robbins calls up all students who earned a mastery stamp in their goal tracker. Those students lead the class in a chant to celebrate the accomplishment, turning growth into a joyful, community-centered moment.

In the final scenario, teams at a high school ensure that each assessment has a cover page that indicates the standards being assessed. As a result, when students do not show mastery on the essential standards as measured by the end-of-unit assessment, teams of teachers analyze their student work, focusing on the items or questions that measured those essential standards. Then, based on the errors or misconceptions students revealed, teacher teams develop instructional strategies and plans to address those errors for groups of students that share the same need. Teachers execute the Tier 2 intervention during the designated time. They ensure students reflect so they know the learning their Tier 2 intervention time will target. In this school, each content area had a designated two days every two weeks. So, teams organized their analysis of their end-of-unit assessment evidence to design this targeted intervention.

In this scenario, Mrs. White is starting her first session of intervention with a group of students and is taking the time to review the assessment cover page.

Mrs. White: Quickly find a seat, please. We are going to review the results of your last unit assessment in Biology. I have each of your assessments and the completed cover page. Take a minute to review your results and feedback. Turn and talk to the person next to you and tell them something you did well.

Over the next two weeks, we will work specifically in the areas that your cover page shows need improvement. I will give multiple opportunities for you to retest in those areas to help improve your initial grade, but more importantly, provide evidence that you've mastered those skills. I want you to take the time to celebrate and set some goals for this intervention cycle. I will pass out two sticky notes. Identify your celebrations on one and your goals on the other. I will post these notes in the front of the room. When you reach your goals, you can tear up the sticky note and throw it around the room like confetti to celebrate.

Simply by starting intervention getting timely feedback, as well as having time to reflect and set goals, students are developing clarity on where they are going, where they are currently, and what comes next to help them achieve their goal. See figure 4.2 for an example of an assessment cover page.

Name: ____________________________________

Criteria	Questions	Points	Confidence (Check One)
Accurately interprets data on trait variation using statistical measures	Q1, Q2	☐ Correct calculation or identification (5) ☐ Accurate explanation or interpretation (5)	☐ Confident ☐ Unsure ☐ Guessed
Applies probability concepts (for example, Punnett squares, percentages, ratios) to predict outcomes	Q3, Q4	☐ Accurate setup (Punnett, ratio, or mathematics) (5) ☐ Correct probability or logic explained (5)	☐ Confident ☐ Unsure ☐ Guessed
Communicates clearly with evidence, using visuals like histograms or scatterplots	Q5	☐ Correct construction of graph (5) ☐ Clear written explanation of data (5)	☐ Confident ☐ Unsure ☐ Guessed
Explains logically how genetics and environment shape population traits	Q6	☐ Includes both genetics and environment (5) ☐ Logical explanation with evidence (5)	☐ Confident ☐ Unsure ☐ Guessed

Connects learning to meaningful biological contexts beyond the classroom	Q7	☐ Real-world context identified (5) ☐ Accurate explanation using variation and probability (5)	☐ Confident ☐ Unsure ☐ Guessed

Scoring: Each criterion = 10 points (Total: 50). Mastery = 40/50 (80 percent or higher).

Strengths:

Criterion needing intervention (didn't meet mastery):

Action to learn:

Figure 4.2: Biology—Genetics cover page example.

Each scenario, while different in nature, provides creative examples of how you can make students as much a part of the process as teachers when it comes to understanding the grade-level expectation of essential standards. Creating this awareness for students takes the guesswork out of what they are intended to learn. In addition to awareness, specific feedback conversations provide the opportunity to continuously encourage and make students believe that can achieve high levels of learning.

Are You Ready?

Student investment is an essential part of Tier 2 intervention. To set students up for learning more, becoming more independent, and feeling more confident in meeting grade-level essential standards, assessment evidence and instruction must be rooted in learning. Consider the extent in your context that teachers and teams are sharing learning targets and standards with students throughout instruction. Ask yourself the following questions.

- Have teacher teams checked in with students about how confident they are that what they're doing in class links to learning targets?

- To what extent have teachers taught students to reflect and act on feedback?
- Are there structures in place for students to track their learning and progress on essential standards?

Developing a culture where students are invested in their learning is a process and requires teams to try different strategies and monitor their impact. The goal is to find the strategy, the tool, or the process that leads to students being more confident in their learning and showing growth and achievement of the intended learning.

After your team has assessed your readiness, use the reflection questions in the reproducible tool "Pause and Take Action: Chapter 4" to determine the next steps to build your Tier 2 intervention system.

Fostering student ownership requires an instructional approach that encourages student investment in meeting their grade-level goals. When students feel connected to the learning outcomes and have a teacher who encourages and celebrates their incremental goals, acceleration for closing achievement disparities is a natural result. But what happens when learning dispositions remain a problem? How do you pinpoint academic behaviors holding students back from proficiency? We will address these question in the next chapter, where we unpack how cultivating learning dispositions provides students with the mindset to believe they can accomplish their goals.

Pause and Take Action: Chapter 4

Consider the following questions to determine your teacher team's next student ownership actions.

- How does our team ensure students know what the learning target is and what proficiency looks like? What strategies might we implement to make it clearer?
- How do collaborative teams ask students to reflect on their assessment intervention? To what extent do students understand the learning targeted during Tier 2 intervention? What actions might we take to increase student understanding?
- What additional strategies might help students reflect and address the three questions: Where am I going? Where am I now? How do I close the gap?
- How do our teams collectively respond to, inform, and design Tier 2 interventions? Do we make student ownership strategies a critical part of the implementation of the instruction? What adjustments do we need to make, if any?
- How do our teams check our students' experience of their targeted Tier 2 instruction? How do we gauge whether it is building both students' achievement and confidence?
- How do teams gather feedback on students' perceptions of Tier 2 intervention? Do students explicitly describe the intervention as helpful? Do they indicate they believe they can do it?

Team Action Steps

Now that you've reflected, identify two strengths in your teacher team practice related to building student ownership.

Identify two steps your team will take to build more ownership and when those steps will occur.

Second Helpings © 2027 Solution Tree Press • SolutionTree.com
Visit **go.SolutionTree.com/RTIatWork** to download this free reproducible.

CHAPTER 5

Cultivating Learning Dispositions

Imagine sitting down to a meal that's already pretty good, like a tender roast chicken, perfectly cooked vegetables, maybe a warm bread roll or two. But then, someone passes you a small dish of homemade gravy. You try it. Suddenly, the flavors pop. Everything on the plate comes together. That's what learning dispositions are for instruction. They're not the main dish—they're the secret sauce. They're what takes a solid lesson and turns it into something unforgettable. These dispositions are not merely supplemental; they are essential ingredients for student success, both in and out of the classroom. Learning dispositions are what make students able to transfer learning from situation to situation over time.

Effective Tier 1 instruction gives every student access to high-quality content. National, state, provincial, and district assessments are essential for determining whether students meet established academic standards. While these assessments provide valuable data, they often fail to capture a more comprehensive view of student readiness for the world beyond K–12 school. In the 21st century, it's not enough for students to simply acquire knowledge; they must also learn how to think critically, manage themselves emotionally, and persevere through setbacks. That's where learning dispositions come into play. We might notice instances where a student who demonstrates the necessary skills shuts down at the first sign of a challenge. Or another who starts strong on new tasks but never finishes them. Or a quiet student who frequently demonstrates high-level proficiency when working in isolation but struggles in and avoids group work like the plague. What's missing? Often, it's not ability but a disposition. The mindset. The habits. The internal voice that says, "This is hard, but I can do hard things."

That's where Tier 2 comes in. Dispositions such as self-regulation, metacognition, and perseverance, sometimes referred to as *grit*, allow students to interact meaningfully with their environment, persist in facing difficulties, and develop a reflective approach to learning. These habits of mind equip students to actively pursue knowledge with curiosity and resilience. Rapid technological changes define society and such qualities are no longer optional; they are necessary for academic success and lifelong adaptability.

In this chapter, we'll explore how intentionally cultivating learning dispositions, such as perseverance, self-regulation, metacognition, and a growth mindset (the belief that one's actions help one grow), can completely change the learning experience. We also offer practical ways you can integrate these dispositions into classroom instruction, particularly within the RTI framework. Building these into Tier 2 support means we're not just helping students pass a test—we're helping them build the skills to tackle life.

The Purpose of Cultivating Learning Dispositions

Let's be real: The world students are walking into doesn't look like the one many teachers grew up in. Content knowledge still matters, but so do curiosity, emotional intelligence, persistence, and the ability to problem solve when there's no straightforward answer. Students need to be able to think about their thinking, bounce back from setbacks, and stay focused when things get tough.

Traditional instruction often focuses on the *what* of learning. Dispositions concentrate on the *how*. How do I keep going when I get stuck? How do I know if I truly understand this? How do I handle the frustration of not getting it yet? Learning dispositions allow students to take their learning from the classroom and apply it anywhere. That's why learning dispositions are essential, not extra.

In their book *Behavior Solutions: Teaching Academic and Social Skills Through RTI at Work*, John Hannigan, Jessica Djabrayan Hannigan, Mike Mattos, and Austin Buffum (2021) offer a comprehensive framework for addressing student behavior through an instructional and preventive lens. Rather than treating behavior and academics as separate domains, the authors advocate for integrating social-emotional learning and academic instruction within a tiered RTI structure. Central to their approach is the understanding that many student behavior challenges do not result from disobedience but instead reflect deficits of skills that can, and should, be taught explicitly within the school day.

Hannigan and colleagues (2021) reframe academic behaviors as *learning dispositions*, meaning the tendencies or habits of mind influencing how students engage with learning tasks. According to Hannigan and colleagues, multiple dispositions directly affect academic and behavioral success. These dispositions are not innate traits but can be developed through intentional teaching and practice. By equipping students with these key dispositions, educators create environments where students are more likely to succeed academically and socially. *Behavior Solutions* provides practical tools, rubrics, and protocols for identifying behavior skill gaps and explicitly teaching replacement behaviors and life skills. These include strategies for promoting self-regulation, task completion, cooperation, and respectful communication. Table 5.1 describes academic and social behaviors that Hannigan and colleagues (2021) articulate as critical to student success.

Table 5.1: Essential Academic and Social Behaviors

Academic Behaviors	Social Behaviors
In addition to academic skills and knowledge, some academic behaviors are critical to school and career success.	Success in school and career requires the ability to consistently demonstrate socially appropriate behaviors.
Metacognition: Knowledge and beliefs about thinking **Self-concept:** A student's belief in their abilities **Self-monitoring:** The ability to plan and prepare for learning **Motivation:** The ability to initiate and maintain interest in tasks **Strategy:** Techniques for organizing and memorizing knowledge **Volition:** The efforts and techniques needed to stay motivated and engaged in learning (Many educators refer to this as demonstrating *grit*.)	**Responsible verbal and physical interactions with peers and adults:** Skills that demonstrate social responsibility, honesty, compassion, respect, self-regulation, and self-control **Appropriate language:** Skills that demonstrate self-awareness, communication, civility, and character **Respect for property and materials:** Skills that demonstrate empathy and respect **Independently staying on a required task:** Skills that demonstrate on-task behavior **Regular attendance:** Skills that demonstrate punctuality, time management, and accountability

Source: Adapted from Hannigan et al., 2021, p. 53.

Cultivating student dispositions is far more than a classroom management strategy; it's an investment in students' long-term well-being and success. While these dispositions may support smoother learning experiences day to day, their true power lies in preparing students for life beyond school, including postsecondary education, the workplace, and life.

- **In postsecondary education:** Students are expected to manage their schedules, meet academic expectations independently, and cope with the emotional challenges of a new environment. Dispositions like self-regulation and metacognition enable students to plan ahead, monitor their own progress, and adapt to the demands of higher education. These skills are often the difference between thriving and merely surviving in a college setting.
- **In the workplace:** Employees encounter constant change, whether through evolving technologies, shifting team dynamics, or new expectations. Having a growth mindset enables individuals to embrace challenges, learn from feedback, and continue to develop professionally. Dispositions like motivation, collaboration, and responsibility are essential for success in modern careers.
- **In life:** Setbacks are inevitable. Whether facing personal loss, financial hardship, or failure, individuals with grit and volition are more likely to recover and persevere. Teaching these dispositions helps students become adaptable, confident adults who can navigate uncertainty with courage, resilience, and a sense of purpose.

When students learn important dispositions, it does more than help them succeed in school; it prepares them for real life. These traits give students the tools they need to handle whatever they encounter in life.

In their book *Teaching Self-Regulation*, Amy S. Gaumer Erickson and Patricia M. Noonan (2022) define *self-regulation* as a set of skills that helps students control impulses, set and work toward goals, and make thoughtful decisions. These skills enable students to manage their behaviors and emotions, even in challenging situations, ultimately supporting them in becoming more independent learners. Self-regulation is crucial because it enables students to take charge of their behaviors. Students who can self-regulate can be OK even when they experience strong emotions and remain mindful of their environment, thoughts, and bodies.

Hannigan and colleagues (2021) explore the crucial role of self-regulation in helping students engage with learning tasks more effectively. Gaumer Erickson and

Noonan (2022) note that self-regulated students are better at managing frustration, staying on task, and persisting through difficulties. Teaching self-regulation can improve academic performance and build resilience. It also fosters a greater sense of agency; students begin to recognize that they have the power to influence their outcomes through the choices they make. This sense of ownership and confidence can be transformative, particularly for students who may have struggled with behavioral or emotional regulation in the past. Gaumer Erickson and Noonan (2022) write that self-regulation is essential for lifelong learning, and teaching it gives students skills they can use to succeed in every area of their lives. Whether they are navigating academic tasks, peer interactions, or everyday stressors, self-regulation gives students the tools they need to thrive.

Perseverance, or grit, is also required of students for overcoming challenges and staying focused on long-term objectives. Grit makes a student more likely to persevere in the face of challenges and failures, which is essential for individual and academic success. When displaying grit, students must believe in their worth, always keep practicing and trying, maintain a positive attitude, and give their best effort at all times.

In her book *Grit: The Power of Passion and Perseverance*, Angela Duckworth (2016) argues that grit, a combination of effort, passion, and perseverance, plays a far more critical role in achieving success than talent or intelligence alone. Duckworth's research concludes that grit better predicts success than talent alone. Success is not just about natural ability but about hard work, dedication, and the ability to keep going in the face of adversity.

Students with grit understand that failure is not the end, it's part of the journey. They view setbacks as opportunities to learn and grow rather than reasons to give up. Developing grit encourages students to set goals that matter to them and commit to those goals even when the path gets difficult. As Duckworth (2016) explains:

> Grit is passion and perseverance for very long-term goals. Grit is having stamina. Grit is sticking with your future, day in, day out, not just for the week, not just for the month, but for years, and working hard to make that future a reality. (p. 8)

Instilling grit in students not only helps them succeed in school but also prepares them to face life's challenges with determination and resilience.

When we think about grit, it is important to be mindful that we don't always see the full story. For some students, especially those dealing with trauma, bullying, or difficult home situations, just walking through the school doors on time each day takes grit. What may look like a lack of effort in the classroom might actually reflect energy already spent outside of school. As educators, we need to keep this perspective in mind and recognize that grit can look very different from one student to the next. By noticing and valuing this resilience, we can better support students and build on the grit they already show.

A growth mindset is the belief that someone can develop abilities, intelligence, and talents over time through effort, practice, and perseverance. Developed by psychologist Carol S. Dweck (2016), the concept of a growth mindset allows people to view challenges as opportunities for growth, embrace effort as a path to improvement, and see mistakes as valuable learning experiences.

Dweck (2016) concludes that mindsets profoundly shape how we approach life, learning, and success. People with a growth mindset achieve more because they understand that success is not fixed or predetermined—it's earned through dedication and resilience. They're more likely to persist through difficulties, try new strategies when things get tough, and actively seek feedback to improve.

When students develop a growth mindset, they become more willing to take academic risks, more confident in their ability to improve, and more resilient when they experience setbacks. This mindset doesn't ignore failure; it redefines it. Rather than being a sign of limitation, failure becomes a stepping-stone toward mastery. Dweck (2016) notes that with a growth mindset, the value lies in the work, not just in the outcome—tackling problems, charting new courses, and working on important issues are meaningful. By fostering a growth mindset, educators help students not just succeed in school but thrive far beyond it.

Metacognition is becoming one of the most essential skills for students to master. Students who can think about their thinking are more capable of higher-level cognition. For students, metacognition is more than memorizing; it requires them to apply and generalize their learned knowledge. It encourages self-awareness and reflective habits that empower students to become more strategic and intentional in their learning.

Webb (2021) offers practical insights into incorporating metacognition into classroom teaching and school leadership. Webb finds that metacognitive strategies significantly enhance learning outcomes. Students who know their learning processes are better equipped to retain information, adapt to new challenges, and improve problem-solving skills.

When students learn to monitor their thinking, such as recognizing when they don't understand something or knowing which strategies help them learn best, they gain greater control over their academic success. Teaching metacognition helps students understand what they learn and how they learn, building independence and resilience. As Webb (2021) writes, "Teaching students how to think about their thinking can transform their ability to learn independently. It's the key to unlocking lifelong learning" (p. 15). Helping students develop metacognitive awareness gives them the tools to become more reflective, confident, and capable learners.

Learning Dispositions in Action

In a busy classroom, dispositions show up in all kinds of subtle ways. A student who pauses to ask herself, "What strategy worked for me last time?" is using metacognition. A student who takes a few deep breaths instead of tearing up a mathematics paper in frustration is practicing self-regulation. A student who chooses to keep working through a tough science project, even after failing the first attempt, is showing grit. But these behaviors often don't come naturally, especially for students who've struggled or who believe that learning just isn't their thing. That's why Tier 2 support focused on dispositions can be so powerful. It's where teachers explicitly name, model, and teach the habits of mind that help students engage with learning in a deeper, lasting way. Integrating learning dispositions into classroom instruction doesn't mean adding more to an already full plate. Here are examples of how this can be done across different grade levels.

- **Grades K–2:** Teachers use stories to discuss emotions and appropriate responses, role-play social scenarios, and practice mindfulness with short breathing exercises.
- **Grades 3–5:** Students reflect on learning processes through journals, use emotion charts to track their feelings, and set short-term goals for academic tasks.
- **Grades 6–8:** Teachers incorporate self-assessments and student-led conferences to build metacognition. Grit is discussed in the context of famous historical figures or scientists who overcame obstacles.
- **Grades 9–12:** Students analyze their learning data, use peer feedback for growth, and explore case studies of professional success tied to perseverance and adaptability.

So, what does teaching learning dispositions look like in practice? In a Tier 2 setting, you have the perfect opportunity to slow down and focus on the *how* of learning, not just the *what*. In these small groups, typically three to six students, you can create a space for guided conversations, modeling, and practice around the dispositions. This setting encourages students to learn from one another, celebrate progress, and apply strategies such as the following in a supportive environment before transferring them back to the whole-class setting.

- **Mindfulness and emotional regulation:** Start your small group with a minute of breathing or a simple check-in. Teach students that calming down their minds is the first step in getting ready to learn.
- **Positive self-talk:** Many students have negative self-talk, like, "I'm bad at this" or "I'll never get it." Help them rewrite that story. Try journaling prompts like, "One time I kept going even though something was hard was . . ."
- **Grit goals:** Help students set short-term goals that are just beyond their comfort zone. Celebrate not just achievement, but effort—"I saw how you didn't give up even when you got stuck three times. That is showing grit!"
- **Metacognition journals:** After each session, give students a chance to reflect—"What did I learn? What was tricky? What did I do that helped me stay focused or solve a problem?"

When a teacher team notices they have a significant number of students struggling with self-regulation, they need a way for students to define the skills related to success, reflect on them weekly, and set goals to focus their improvement and growth. Self-regulation and organization are closely connected. Self-regulation is a student's ability to manage their thoughts, attention, emotions, and behaviors to reach a goal. Organization is one of the most visible ways this skill appears in school. When students manage their materials, track assignments, plan their time, and structure their work, they are demonstrating self-regulation in action. In this way, organization is not simply a study habit but a practical expression of a student's ability to regulate their learning. For example, a teacher team completed a three-part assessment of students' progress. First, the team observed and made notes regarding each student's actions according to the criteria in figure 5.1. The second assessment was students' self-reflection on how they demonstrated that skill over the course of the week. The third assessment was of students' progress in the skill (did they show more learning if they demonstrated more of this learning disposition or not?). Tracking tools like the one in figure 5.1 can also help counselors or others who support students in achieving these learning dispositions provide feedback and facilitate conferences.

Name: ____________________

Part 1: Organization Self-Assessment. Use this set of criteria ("I can" statements) to assess what you currently feel confident about and what you want to work on.

Criteria **I can organize my workflow. This means . . .**	**I do this regularly and it works or I'm confident.**	**I do this sometimes.**	**I know this is part of organization but don't do it yet.**	**I'm not sure how to do this or I don't see it as relevant.**
I can find my work in my binder.				
I can put my papers and materials for my classes in order. (This means I can put my papers in a folder labeled by subject.)				
I come to class prepared to learn. (This means I have my pencil, backpack, and Chromebook.)				
I can use time effectively to do the following: Be organized Complete my work Be on time to class				
I can follow along and focus on the task at hand. (This means I can identify strategies such as deep breathing techniques and positive self-talk and use them to focus and refocus.)				

Figure 5.1: Student self-assessment and reflection on organization skills.

continued ▶

Part 2: Weekly Reflection on Organization

Date	What area of organization went well and what example shows that?	What area of organization was harder to do and when did you notice this?	Goal for next week: What are you going to work on?
April 28			
May 5			
May 12			

Visit ***go.SolutionTree.com/RTIatWork*** *for a free reproducible version of this figure.*

Just as with academic learning, helping students strengthen their learning dispositions must be a collaborative effort. No single teacher can meet every academic and behavioral need of every student alone, which is why this work must be collaborative. Teacher teams and the guiding coalition work together to lead the schoolwide Tier 1 effort by identifying and defining the academic and social behaviors all students should learn and develop during their time at the school. The guiding coalition helps establish the shared vision and priorities, while teacher teams implement, reinforce, and monitor those expectations in their classrooms. Through this shared responsibility, schools create consistent support for developing both the academic skills and learning dispositions students need to succeed.

While these skills cross grade level and course, they may look a little different in different grade levels or courses. However, the entire school plays a role in ensuring students learn these skills. At Tier 2, the guiding coalition partners with counselors, specialists, or social-emotional behavior teams to provide the additional feedback, instruction, and support for students who need to work on those targeted essential learning dispositions. And don't forget to bring families into the conversation. Many families are eager to support these habits at home but just need a little guidance and support. The guiding coalition can help facilitate what that support looks like with the partners who have that expertise.

Are You Ready?

The world is unpredictable, and knowing how to bounce back from challenges, work well with others, and think through problems calmly is just as important as knowing how to solve an equation or write an essay. By helping students build these habits early, you can help them grow into capable, confident adults who can navigate the world with confidence and resilience. Some students walk into the classroom already equipped with strong dispositions. Others don't, and that is OK too. It doesn't mean they're lazy or unmotivated. It means they need you to explicitly teach the tools that other students may have picked up more naturally. Tier 2 isn't about labeling students. It's about responding with care, intention, and a laser focus. When you notice that a student shuts down at the first sign of difficulty, don't assume they're incapable. Assume they're missing a tool and give it to them.

Learning dispositions do not always appear on a report card, but they are evident in how a student approaches challenges, responds to mistakes, and believes in their ability to improve. Just as the best meals are not defined only by the main dish, learning is not only about content. It is also about the experience, the confidence students develop, and the internal drive that keeps them engaged and willing to try again. When teachers intentionally nurture learning dispositions within Tier 2 support, they give students more than strategies. They help students develop the persistence and confidence needed to continue learning beyond a single lesson or school year.

As you plan your next small-group session, consider not only the skills students need but also the dispositions that will help them grow. Ask yourself, "What habits, mindsets, or behaviors do my students need right now, and how can I help them practice those in meaningful ways?" When you intentionally weave these elements into intervention, students gain both the skills and the resilience needed to succeed.

After your team has assessed your readiness, use the reflection questions in the reproducible tool "Pause and Take Action: Chapter 5" (page 114) to determine the next steps to build your Tier 2 intervention system.

Of course, even the strongest interventions require time and structure within the school day. In the next chapter, we will explore how schools design a master schedule that makes this work possible, ensuring that time for Tier 2 support is intentional, protected, and accessible for all students.

Pause and Take Action: Chapter 5

Consider the following questions to determine your teacher team's next student learning disposition actions.

- Which learning dispositions do we believe are most essential for students' success? Why do we consider these the most important?
- What are some challenges students might face in developing strong learning dispositions? How can we help them overcome these challenges?
- Who in our building is best suited to guide teaching these skills and collaboratively respond when students need more time and support to achieve these dispositions?
- How can our guiding coalition and administration support or guide teams to take action if they need support?
- Has our guiding coalition facilitated an intentional discussion across our school so all people in the building, including teacher teams, are clear about a common vision for learning dispositions? Do we have a set of academic and social behaviors that everyone in the school embraces and commits to teaching and promoting?
- How might teaching and cultivating learning dispositions impact students' long-term academic and personal success?

Team Action Steps

Now that you've reflected, identify two strengths in your teacher team practice related to the importance of learning dispositions.

Identify two next steps your team will take to further develop learning dispositions instruction and implementation and when those steps will occur.

Second Helpings © 2027 Solution Tree Press • SolutionTree.com
Visit **go.SolutionTree.com/RTIatWork** to download this free reproducible.

CHAPTER 6

Designing a Master Schedule That Serves Every Learner

In any well-functioning kitchen, meal preparation doesn't end when the first plates are served. In fact, in some cases, a meal must be ready to be served multiple times if family members or guests have varying schedules; everyone needs to be fed, and some will need more than others. Thoughtful chefs know that not every person finishes dinner satisfied with a single serving. Some will need a second helping. However, unlike a kitchen, where additional servings are available on request, providing the Tier 2 intervention that is the second helping in schools is often contingent on complicated factors such as time, staffing, space, and, most importantly, the master schedule.

Too often, schools are structured in ways that make Tier 2 support feel like an afterthought, as it is usually squeezed into lunch periods, after-school hours, or taken from electives or core instruction. When schools strive to commit to equity and support for all learners, their master schedule must reflect that commitment. This means intentionally building in time for all three tiers of instruction within the daily school routines.

This chapter explores how to set the table for all students by creating a master schedule that anticipates and provides space for differentiated servings of support. Whether at the elementary, middle, or high school level, this work is essential for ensuring that no student gets left out of learning. The guiding coalition plays a critical role in shaping the master schedule by protecting time for strong Tier 1 core instruction, building in dedicated intervention and enrichment blocks for Tiers 2 and 3, and safeguarding collaborative team time. The guiding coalition also helps align staffing to student needs and ensures equity across grade levels and departments. Because the master schedule reflects the school's priorities, it should be developed collaboratively by those leading the improvement effort rather than created in isolation. While the principal may finalize the schedule, the guiding coalition ensures it aligns with the school's mission, tiered supports, and collective commitments.

The Purpose of a Well-Designed Master Schedule

A master schedule is more than a logistic tool; it is a values statement that reveals more transparently than any mission statement what a school believes is most important. It reflects priorities, including instructional time, who has access to key staff, and which student needs are considered central versus supplementary. If schools claim to value every learner, especially those who require additional support, then their master schedule must include protected time for intervention and enrichment. Without this, there is no commitment to equity, and the promise that students will achieve at grade level and beyond, no matter what, evaporates. A schedule that only accommodates Tier 1 instruction is not built for equity. It's built for efficiency. And when efficiency outweighs equity, students who require more support are often the ones who suffer the most.

Schedules that fail to prioritize Tier 2 or Tier 3 instruction with purpose and clarity send a dangerous and inequitable message: "We will help you, but only if it fits our schedule." This approach puts the responsibility on students to adapt to a system that is not designed with their needs in mind. It frames interventions as optional extras rather than essential supports and unintentionally signals that only some students are fully valued in the schedule. A student-centered schedule ensures that extra help and enrichment are a built-in, visible, and non-negotiable part of the learning process.

On the surface, pulling students for interventions during recess, lunch, or electives is a quick fix. However, these scheduling decisions create unintended consequences that disproportionately affect the very students who rely on school the most. They send subtle yet powerful messages, such as the following.

- "You don't get to be in the play because you need reading fluency help."
- "You can't explore coding because you're in math intervention."
- "You're missing art today because you're low in comprehension."

Over time, these kinds of experiences add up, and students start to feel like they have to give up the parts of school they enjoy, such as art, music, clubs, or time with friends, just to get the help they need. It can start to feel like they're being punished for needing extra support.

There's a difference between saying all students *can* receive support and actually making time for them to get it. This is where the master schedule becomes the driving force in ensuring all students get what they need. When schools ensure that time for supplemental and intensive instruction is embedded, protected, and normalized in the master schedule, they provide students not just opportunity, but access. Equity does not begin with programming; it begins with access, and access is what levels the playing field.

Here's the reality: Intervention is instruction. It is not separate, optional, or lesser. Tier 2 isn't a break from learning because it *is* learning. It is highly focused, data-driven, and skill-specific teaching designed to close gaps, accelerate progress, and rebuild confidence. When delivered with intention, Tier 2 instruction helps students reconnect to learning by addressing the very things they didn't understand the first time around.

When schools make space for second helpings in the schedule, they send a clear message to students: "We know what you need, and we're prepared to give it to you without making you sacrifice something else in return." This lets students know they matter and that their teachers believe they can succeed. It honors the fact that needing more time or more instruction is not a deficit; it is a normal and expected part of learning. Designing a schedule that honors all three tiers of instruction requires the following.

- **Data-informed groupings:** Schedules must be flexible enough to adjust based on student data. That means reassessing regularly and moving students in and out of support groups as needed.
- **Shared ownership:** All staff, not just interventionists, must take responsibility for Tier 2 instruction. The schedule should reflect that shared responsibility, with general education teachers involved in planning and delivery.
- **Protected time:** Intervention time must be sacred. It should not be lost to assemblies, testing, or meetings. If it's optional or routinely canceled, students receive inconsistent access.

- **Leadership commitment:** Principals and schedulers must treat the inclusion of all three tiers in the schedule as non-negotiable. It's not a luxury; it's the foundation of equitable education.

When schools put their commitments into action, the master schedule shows what they truly value. The real test is not just having good ideas, but making sure those ideas are part of everyday routines. A strong schedule makes it easy to plan interventions, protects time for teachers to work together, and ensures support is consistent. It also builds in extra time and help for students during the school day so no one has to rely on luck or someone being available.

The Master Schedule in Action

Setting up a strong tiered support system helps schools start with general time guidelines. The exact number of minutes depends on the grade, but we recommend adding twenty to forty minutes each day for Tier 2 focusing on essential standards. For students who need Tier 3 support in foundational reading, writing, or numeracy skills, that support must be in addition to, not in place of, Tier 1 and 2 instruction. Tier 3 usually means forty-five to sixty minutes of daily instruction, often in smaller groups or one on one. Tier 3 may be broken into two sessions per day, such as twenty-five minutes in the morning and an additional twenty-five minutes in the afternoon.The main idea is that the intervention supplements Tier 1 instruction and Tier 2 intervention; it does not replace it.

Schedule Tier 2 and Tier 3 time blocks separately so they do not overlap. Some students will need both kinds of support, so clear separation ensures no interventions are skipped or limited. The master schedule needs to be designed so that each support layer builds on the previous one, avoiding conflicts. Designing a master schedule that includes Tier 2 and Tier 3 supports is a leadership responsibility and a guiding coalition action. It cannot be delegated or delayed. It must be a foundational component of school planning that begins not with software but with the following set of core questions.

- Who are our most vulnerable learners?
- When during the day will they receive what they need?
- Who will provide that instruction?
- How will we ensure that support is not contingent on loss of electives, recess, and so on?
- What structural changes will we make to protect intervention time from disruption?

These questions do not have easy answers. They require trade-offs, collaboration, and problem solving. But when leadership makes including Tier 2 and Tier 3 instruction non-negotiable, the schedule becomes something that meets students' needs instead of something that holds them back.

The following examples provide places to start that you can use to facilitate discussion about your current scheduling reality. In addition, you will find many examples on the www.allthingsplc.info website. You can search for schools of your same size and demographics and reach out to their leadership for copies of their master schedules. In addition, the books *It's About Time: Planning Interventions and Extensions in Elementary School* (Buffum & Mattos, 2015) and *It's About Time: Planning Interventions and Extensions in Secondary School* (Mattos & Buffum, 2015) can provide other resources for intentionally and effectively building schedules and making time.

Elementary School

In elementary schools, the most effective way to provide Tier 2 instruction is through a daily intervention and enrichment block, often called WIN ("what I need") time. This dedicated time, typically thirty to forty-five minutes, occurs outside of core instruction and is used flexibly to respond to student data, often end-of-unit assessments that measure where students are in achieving essential standards. This time is focused on essential standards and not all learning or general help.

The following are key features of an elementary schedule that supports all three tiers.

- **Protected WIN time:** The schedule includes "What I need" time every day, with no new core instruction during this block.
- **All hands on deck:** Every available adult (such as interventionists, instructional aides, special education teachers, and literacy coaches) participates to reduce group sizes and meet diverse needs.
- **Fluid groupings:** Groupings are based on current data, not static labels. Students might receive Tier 2 support in reading during one cycle and enrichment in mathematics the next.

In figure 6.1 (page 120), the schedule for the elementary school day begins with morning work and a class meeting to build community. Literacy instruction includes phonics, fluency, and interactive read-alouds. Students work in centers and small groups for independent practice, Tier 2 instruction, and any needed Tier 3 supports. Mathematics includes whole-group Tier 1 instruction with time for Tier 2 and Tier 3 supports. WIN time provides additional intervention or enrichment

7:45–8:15	Morning work Class meeting
8:15–9:00	Phonics and fluency
9:05–9:30	Interactive read-aloud or shared reading
9:30–10:30	Learning centers and small-group rotations • Independent practice • Tier 2 groups • Tier 3 push-in or pull-out support
10:30–11:00	Writing
11:10–12:00	Lunch and recess
12:00–1:00	Mathematics • 40 minutes: Tier 1 • 20 minutes: Tier 2 groups, Tier 3 push-in support
1:05–1:30	WIN time
1:30–1:50	Recess
2:00–2:50	Specials: PE, music, art, library, STEM lab Professional learning team time

Figure 6.1: Elementary sample master schedule.

based on each student's needs. During specials (for example, music, art, PE) teachers have time to collaborate in professional learning teams. This schedule protects time for core instruction, intervention, and enrichment so every student is supported. The schedule also includes time for short breaks, but build these in however works best for your situation.

By embedding a daily support block into the master schedule, elementary schools ensure that second helpings are not dependent on students being pulled from core subjects or recess and instead ensure everyone gets what they need.

Middle School

Middle schools present unique scheduling challenges due to departmentalization, bell schedules, and an increased number of extracurricular offerings. However, successful secondary schools make intervention work by creating flexible but structured opportunities for targeted support. The following are strategies for integrating tiers into the middle school schedules.

- **Intervention period or advisory block:** Many schools embed a thirty-to-forty-five-minute block once or twice daily dedicated to Tier 2 and Tier 3 instruction. Some use advisory or homeroom time; others schedule it between core classes.

- **Double dosing:** In some cases, students receive an additional period of instruction in reading or mathematics (such as reading workshop or mathematics lab) without sacrificing their elective options. This requires creative scheduling and belief in the importance of second servings without punishment. This second serving is explicitly designated Tier 2 (for more time on grade-level essentials) or Tier 3 (for time on foundational skills).
- **Push-in models:** Interventionists or coteachers join core classes to provide small-group support within the classroom and can be especially integral to facilitating Tier 2 intervention.
- **Team collaboration time:** Grade-level teams or subject-area departments meet regularly to review data and plan targeted supports; this should also be built into the schedule.

In the middle school sample schedule in figure 6.2, students begin to move from class to class. Students move into a science block before an extended ELA block that combines whole-group reading and writing instruction with independent practice, Tier 2 small groups, and push-in Tier 3 support. The mathematics block provides Tier 1 instruction along with additional time for Tier 2 and Tier 3 interventions. WIN time ensures targeted intervention and extension remain a priority for all students. This structure balances Tier 1 instruction with intentional support and enrichment, making sure every learner has protected access to what they need.

7:45–8:15	Homeroom • Spiral review bell ringer • Attendance • Class meeting
8:15–9:00	Science
9:05–11:05	ELA block • 40 minutes: Tier 1 reading • 45 minutes: independent practice, rotating • Tier 2 groups and Tier 3 push-in • 35 minutes: Tier 1 writing
11:10–12:10	Lunch and team time
12:15–1:15	Math block • 40 minutes: Tier 1 • 20 minutes: additional Tier 2 and Tier 3 push-in

Figure 6.2: Middle school sample master schedule.

continued ▶

1:15–1:40	WIN (intervention and extension priority)
1:45–2:45	Specials: PE, music, art, library Professional learning team time
2:50–3:00	Homeroom • Pack up • Dismissal

What matters most is making support a normal part of the school day and not something students have to sign up for, earn through someone's opinion, or only get after school. When middle schools build this support into their schedule, it sends the message that everyone needs a second helping now and then, and that is OK!

High School

High schools often have the most rigid schedules and the least flexibility for intervention. Credit requirements, graduation pathways, and course offerings can make it seem impossible to embed Tier 2 support without pulling students from electives or doubling core classes. But *impossible* is not a word used by schools that value equity.

Following are some solutions for integrating tiered support into the high school schedule.

- **Academic flex periods:** Also known as WIN time, reassessment, tutoring, or enrichment, these are short blocks built into the day (often thirty minutes) for targeted interventions. Some schools use them daily; others use them a few times per week.
- **Extended learning periods:** A few schools extend certain class periods (for example, English 9 or Algebra I) to allow built-in intervention without the need for a second course. These "lab" classes are cotaught or supported by interventionists.
- **RTI electives:** Some high schools create intervention courses that carry elective credit but focus on essential academic skills and dispositions. This approach helps reduce the stigma often associated with intervention and gives students more choice in their schedules. Importantly, these courses are not a replacement for required Tier 1 core classes, but rather, a supplemental support designed to help students succeed in them. For example, a course like academic strategies may target reading comprehension, executive functioning, and study skills. Other electives, such as mathematics lab or literacy seminar, can offer targeted Tier 2

interventions embedded within engaging formats like project-based learning or college- and career-readiness activities.

- **Virtual or flipped interventions:** Leveraging technology for asynchronous support or flipped instruction can free up time for targeted Tier 2 work during the day.

The sample high school schedule in figure 6.3 includes a WIN intervention block. Teacher teams analyze their end-of-unit assessments and identify students who have not mastered essential standards. Each day includes a priority Tier 2 intervention time for different content, which happens during WIN time (1:10–2:00). If students need more time to learn the essential standards as measured by the end-of-unit assessment on the priority content day, they must go to that teacher and engage in the intervention.

7:30–8:00	Homeroom foundations, breakfast • Direct teaching on learning dispositions and student reflection on work • Graduation planning
8:00–8:50	Hour 1: English
8:55–9:45	Hour 2: Algebra I
9:50–10:40	Hour 3: Biology
10:45–11:40	Hour 4: World history
11:45–12:10	Lunch
12:15–1:05	Hour 5: Elective or Tier 3 acceleration (focused on supporting literacy for texts in other content classes along with direct foundational reading or mathematics instruction)
1:10–2:00	WIN time (flexible for intervention or enrichment)
2:05–2:50	Hour 6: Spanish

Figure 6.3: High school sample master schedule.

Figures 6.4 (page 124), 6.5 (page 125), 6.6 (page 125), and 6.7 (page 126) show example Tier 2 schedules through the week. These schedules include which collaborative teams meet and what they focus on and show the priority content area with teachers names so that Tier 2 intervention can be planned intentionally. They also include flex time for students to receive additional intervention as needed when they don't have a priority essential standard to work on. For example, if a student

Monday, August 26 *Priority will be given to content areas for extension activities and elective classes.*		
Priority	Extension or Elective	*If any of your students need extension or intervention for an elective, please complete the Google form.*
Flex	Mrs. Anderson	
	Mrs. Garcia	
	Mrs. Lopez	
	Mrs. Ferguson	
	Mr. Peters	
	Mrs. Morris	
	Mrs. Loving	
	Mr. Abe	
	Ms. Swan	
	Mrs. Weets	
	Mrs. Hernandez	

Source: © 2025 by Hansen Schools of Hansen, Idaho. Adapted with permission.

Figure 6.4: Schedule for Tier 2 intervention for Mondays at Hansen High School—Electives.

has mastered all the essential mathematics standards on Wednesday, they can go to a teacher listed in the flex column and get support in other content areas. Just as in the earlier grades, high school students need to know that needing help isn't a deficit. In fact, getting help is a strength. When schools schedule support with dignity and flexibility, students are more likely to engage with it and succeed.

Tuesday, August 27 *Priority will be given to teachers for extension activities and elective classes.*		
Team Meetings	Science	*Work on essential standards and then identify learning targets for unit.* *Analyze assessment evidence from student work to identify which students need intervention on the next priority day.* *Analyze the effectiveness of the previous priority intervention.*
	Mrs. Lopez	
	Mrs. Swan	
	Mrs. Weets	
Priority	ELA and Social Studies	*These teachers have priority to request students for interventions.*
	Mrs. Anderson	
	Mrs. Garcia	
	Mr. Peters	*All Government students will demonstrate understanding what the question is asking.*
	Mrs. Loving	*Seventh-grade character POV*
Flex	Mrs. Ferguson	
	Mrs. Morris	
	Mr. Abe	

Source: © 2025 by Hansen Schools of Hansen, Idaho. Adapted with permission.

Figure 6.5: Schedule for Tier 2 intervention for Tuesdays at Hansen High School—ELA and social studies.

Wednesday, August 28 *Priority will be given to content areas for extension activities and elective classes.*		
Team Meetings	ELA and Social Studies	*Work on essential standards and then identify learning targets for unit.* *Analyze assessment evidence from student work to identify which students need intervention on the next priority day.* *Analyze the effectiveness of the previous priority intervention.*
	Mrs. Anderson	
	Ms. Garcia	
	Mr. Peters	
	Mrs. Loving	

Figure 6.6: Schedule for Tier 2 intervention for Wednesdays at Hansen High School—Mathematics.

continued ▶

Priority	Mathematics	*These teachers have priority to request students for interventions*
	Mrs. Ferguson	
	Mrs. Morris	*Solving systems of equations*
	Mr. Abe	
Flex	Mrs. Lopez	*Provide intervention, academic learning opportunities, or study hall*
	Mrs. Swan	
	Mrs. Weets	
	Mrs. Hernandez	

Source: © 2025 by Hansen Schools of Hansen, Idaho. Adapted with permission.

Thursday, August 29 *Priority will be given to content areas for extension activities and elective classes.*		
Team Meetings	Mathematics	*Work on essential standards and then identify learning targets for unit.* *Analyze assessment evidence from student work to identify which students need intervention on the next priority day.* *Analyze the effectiveness of the previous priority intervention.*
	Mrs. Ferguson	
	Mrs. Morris	
	Mr. Abe	
Priority	Science	*These teachers have priority to request students for interventions*
	Mrs. Lopez	*Food science: review unit 1 concepts*
	Mrs. Swan	
	Mrs. Weets	
Flex	Mrs. Anderson	*Provide intervention, academic learning opportunities, or study hall*
	Mrs. Garcia	
	Mr. Peters	
	Mrs. Loving	

Source: © 2025 by Hansen Schools of Hansen, Idaho. Adapted with permission.

Figure 6.7: Schedule for Tier 2 intervention for Thursday at Hansen High School—Science.

These schedules clearly identify essential standards and organize staff support so students receive targeted instruction in specific content areas. They also include built-in flex time, allowing students to access additional intervention when they are not assigned a priority essential standard. When schools structure interventions flexibly, students understand that seeking help is a strength and are more likely to engage and succeed.

Are You Ready?

The master schedule is a true test of a school's commitment to equity because it shows a real promise to help all students learn at high levels. While it's easy for schools to say they want to meet every learner's needs, those needs often go unmet unless they set aside time for students in a clear and fair way. Intervention time shouldn't be seen as an extra that only happens if there's room in the schedule. With careful planning, the master schedule becomes more than just a calendar—it's a promise that every student, no matter where they start, will have the time, access, and opportunity to grow.

In this chapter, we looked at how time, structures, and shared responsibility help build a strong Tier 2 schedule. Even with a great plan, schools face real challenges. Issues like limited staff, other priorities, and old habits can make things difficult. The job isn't finished once the schedule is made. Teams need to keep working together to overcome obstacles and improve their approach, using that time intentionally for targeted intervention. Additionally, they must consistently use data from grade-level assessment evidence to determine what is working and what needs to change to ensure students learn grade-level essential standards.

After your team has assessed your readiness, use the reflection questions in the reproducible tool "Pause and Take Action: Chapter 6" (page 128) to determine the next steps to build your Tier 2 intervention system.

In the next chapter, we'll look at these challenges head-on and share practical solutions to help your team keep up the commitment you've started.

Pause and Take Action: Chapter 6

Consider the following questions to determine your teacher team's next master schedule actions.

- How do we currently build our master schedule? What factors contribute to it being the way it is?
- What hidden messages might our current master schedule send to students about who matters and what matters most?
- In what ways does our master schedule reflect a belief that Tier 2 instruction is essential, not optional?
- If a new staff member looked only at our master schedule, what would they conclude our school values most?
- Based on the criteria articulated in this chapter, how many items on this checklist are part of our current master schedule?
    - ☐ Tier 1 instruction is clearly defined and protected for all students.
    - ☐ Tier 2 time is built into the schedule and not pulled from other critical learning experiences.
    - ☐ Tier 3 supports are intensive and embedded.
    - ☐ The schedule supports students who need all three tiers, and they do not miss Tier 1 core instruction on essential standards or Tier 2 intervention time.
    - ☐ Every grade level or department has dedicated collaboration time to analyze student data from common assessments of grade-level standards. Educators then use that data to make instructional decisions and plan Tier 1 core instruction and Tier 2 intervention.
    - ☐ Support staff (interventionists, specialists, special education teachers, and support for multilingual learners) are scheduled based on student need, not just availability.
    - ☐ The schedule is reviewed quarterly for gaps, conflicts, and accessibility barriers. Assessment evidence is used to identify what is working and what isn't.
    - ☐ Families are informed about how and when their child receives supplemental or intensive support and the expected outcome and progress monitoring.

Team Action Steps

Now that you've reflected, identify two strengths in your teacher team practice related to your master schedule's ability to provide Tier 2 intervention.

Identify two next steps your team will take to assess the effectiveness of your master schedule and when those steps will occur.

Second Helpings © 2027 Solution Tree Press • SolutionTree.com
Visit **go.SolutionTree.com/RTIatWork** to download this free reproducible.

CHAPTER 7

Tackling Challenges and Finding Solutions

Tier 2 instruction is the second helping in the educational experience. It is the extra serving of support that some students need to truly thrive. And just like in a kitchen, preparing that second helping requires the right ingredients, the right timing, and a team that's ready to serve with care and purpose.

But what happens when the kitchen runs out of food? Or when there aren't enough hands to pass out the plates? Or when someone is allergic to what's being served? That's when the cooks must get creative, adjust the recipe, and work together to make sure everyone gets nourished.

The successful implementation of Tier 2 is critical for addressing the needs of students who require additional support beyond core classroom instruction. As we've established, Tier 2 isn't a checkbox or a program; it is a mindset and an intentional process. Implementing Tier 2 effectively is rarely simple, as resources are stretched thin and teachers are juggling packed schedules. And yet, the need remains: Some students don't thrive or achieve with Tier 1 instruction alone, and those students deserve the extra support that changes everything.

In this chapter, which has a different format than the previous ones, we address some of the most pressing challenges of delivering Tier 2 support and get to the heart of the innovative and compassionate strategies that can help you overcome them. As we explore practical ways to overcome the challenges, we also spotlight how to maximize Tier 2 impact through creativity, collaboration, and hard work.

Answering Commonly Asked Questions About Tier 2

Isn't Tier 2 just "extra help"? How do you decide who belongs in a Tier 2 group? What if you don't have enough staff to make groups small and manageable? And how do you know the Tier 2 intervention is working? This section tackles these questions head-on with clear answers and practical strategies.

How quickly should students receive Tier 2 support?

Students should receive Tier 2 support in a timely manner once data indicates they are struggling to meet essential standards. The goal is to respond intentionally so that early misconceptions do not turn into larger or compounded disparities later. Schools that implement Tier 2 intervention systems expeditiously have dedicated Tier 2 time where teacher teams are clear about how to use this time in the flow of their instruction and intervention.

In addition, effective teacher teams have designed end-of-unit assessments by standard or learning target that efficiently tell the team which students need more time on grade-level essentials. Teacher team analysis leads to clearly identifying the students that need Tier 2 intervention and on which essentials. Tier 2 time built into the schedule allows for students to get this intervention while the next unit begins. They aren't missing the next unit because there is targeted time.

Sometimes teacher teams will use common formative assessments to inform Tier 2 intervention, and students will get core Tier 1 instruction and then additional Tier 2 support before the unit ends. Whether it is during or after the unit, the goal of Tier 2 is for students who need additional time on grade-level essentials to get it. Teacher teams often make a calendar that specifies when they will be administering, analyzing, and responding to grade-level essentials, both for Tier 1 and Tier 2. That way, the dedicated time is thoughtfully used and planned with the intent of getting that intervention as quickly and as targeted as possible.

Dedicated time, focused assessment evidence, and a clear calendar of when teams will analyze data and respond all pave the way for Tier 2 intervention to be timely.

When Tier 2 interventions are provided quickly, they function as a proactive support rather than a last resort. Timely intervention communicates to students that the school is paying attention to their learning and is committed to helping them succeed. By responding promptly to student needs, teacher teams can adjust instruction, regroup students, and provide targeted practice before frustration or disengagement begins to take hold.

How do we know who needs it?

Identification starts with assessment evidence that measures knowledge of grade-level essential standards. Teacher teams design or choose end-of-unit assessments that are aligned to standards. Teacher teams analyze end-of-unit assessments and identify students who have not mastered the essential standards as measured by the items or tasks aligned to the essential standards. Sometimes teacher teams use common formative assessments not only to inform Tier 1 instruction but also Tier 2 intervention. The key is that students are working on grade-level essential standards during Tier 2 intervention. The guiding coalition may also use schoolwide tools to catch early signs of academic or behavioral disparities. Regular formative assessments, classroom observations, and team discussions also help flag students who are consistently below benchmarks, struggle with foundational skills, or show signs of disengagement. Importantly, educators should consider social-emotional learning data as well. Sometimes a student's difficulty stems more from issues with emotional regulation, confidence, or peer interactions than purely academic challenges. The end-of-unit assessments and common formative assessments are best used to determine who needs Tier 2 intervention on what essential skill. Teachers can also use observation and awareness of consistent below-grade-level performance to identify students who also need foundational skills support during Tier 3 acceleration. If students need support for foundational skills, the master schedule is built to ensure students can receive both Tier 2 support as they need it and Tier 3 support, not either-or.

How long should students remain in Tier 2?

Students should remain in Tier 2 only as long as they need the additional time and support to master the targeted essential skill or concept. Tier 2 is not intended to be a permanent placement but a temporary layer of support to help students close specific learning gaps. Through regular progress monitoring, teacher teams review student data to determine whether the intervention is helping the student make the expected progress. Sometimes students will receive Tier 2 intervention for a few sessions or weeks; other times the Tier 2 intervention will be for a targeted session or two. It completely depends on the teacher team's essential standard and the identified need. If the essential standard happens over multiple units, Tier 2 may last longer than if the essential standard is more specific and confined to one unit.

If data shows that a student has mastered the essential skill, the student can exit Tier 2. If the student is making progress but has not yet reached proficiency, the team may decide to continue the intervention. In cases where little or no progress is evident, the team may adjust the instructional approach, increase the intensity of support, or consider whether Tier 3 intervention is needed in addition to Tier 2 intervention.

What do we do if we don't have additional staff to help?

Members of the teacher team take the lead in delivering Tier 2 intervention because they are best positioned to support students in achieving grade-level essentials. Additional staff can help with extension and be incredibly helpful in supporting the grade-level or course teacher, but the responsibility for delivering Tier 2 intervention falls to the teacher team. With intentional data analysis and a calendar that clearly identifies when the Tier 2 time will happen, what assessment data will determine which students need intervention, and how the team will check to see if it worked, additional staff are nice but not necessary to make this happen effectively. That's why the data analysis step is absolutely essential. When teams take the time to pinpoint the *exact* skill gaps, they can feel confident that all students in the group, whether there are six or sixteen, truly need the same targeted instruction. Teams are not responding to everything. Tier 2 intervention isn't about ensuring every standard. It is about ensuring grade-level essential standards.

This also means that sometimes the groups get larger. If you're supporting a larger group during WIN time (see page 119), here are some ways to make the most of that time.

- **Minilesson plus flexible release:** Start with a short, focused whole-group minilesson. Then, release students who are closer to proficiency to work independently or in pairs on meaningful practice tasks. Keep students who need more support near you for guided practice, prompting, and scaffolding. Wrap up by pulling the full group back together for feedback and reflection.
- **Layered scaffolding approach:** Design one core task that all students complete but scaffold the support levels. For example, some students might get a graphic organizer, sentence stems, or a worked example to refer to, while others complete the task with minimal support. The teacher models first, then monitors and provides real-time scaffolds based on need. This allows all students to work on the same objective, just with varying levels of access.

How do we know it's working?

Progress monitoring or ongoing checks for understanding are key. Depending on how many sessions students receive Tier 2 intervention, teachers check for growth on grade-level essentials throughout the intervention. Teams will administer another assessment on the targeted grade-level essential standard. If students show mastery, teacher teams know it is working. If the grade-level essential is ongoing and longer lasting, teacher teams may assess every two to three weeks, using quick, skill-aligned assessments to track student growth. If the Tier 2 intervention is shorter, then teacher teams assess during and at the end to determine when students have mastered the essential standard and no longer need to work on that essential standard during Tier 2 time. These checkpoints allow educators to adjust instruction, shift groupings, and refine interventions based on real data. If growth is stagnant, it may signal the need for a different strategy or even a move to gain additional Tier 3 support. When students show improvement, it's an opportunity to celebrate their achievement of the essential standard. Tier 2 is dynamic and responsive to each learner's journey.

When the end-of-unit assessment provides evidence for a grade, it is important not to average the first end-of-unit assessment with the second. Students should receive full credit for their new understanding. Rather than averaging these scores, teacher teams replace the old evidence or score with the new. Essentially, Tier 2 time is the reteaching before students retake an assessment. See *The Handbook for Design in Five* (Dimich & Baker-Busby, 2026) for more specific information regarding how to implement this effectively.

How do special education and multilingual teachers fit into Tier 2 systems?

In a strong Tier 2 system, special education teachers and multilingual specialists are not separate from the intervention process—they are essential collaborative partners within it. Their role is not to operate as a parallel system of support but to bring specialized expertise into the team process that designs and delivers targeted instruction for students who need additional time and support. Special educators and multilingual specialists contribute to this system in several important ways.

- **Collaborative problem solving:** Special educators and multilingual specialists participate in team conversations to analyze assessment evidence, identify patterns in student misconceptions, and help determine which students need additional support beyond Tier 1 instruction.

- **Ensuring access to grade-level learning:** Multilingual specialists help teams determine whether a challenge is related to language development or conceptual understanding and help design scaffolds that ensure students can access academic content.
- **Aligning interventions with IEP supports:** For students with individualized education programs (IEPs), special educators play a key role in helping teams align Tier 2 supports with the services, accommodations, and instructional approaches identified in the IEP. This alignment ensures that the interventions students receive reinforce both grade-level expectations and the individualized supports required for them to access learning. Aligning IEPs and 504 plans can be incredibly helpful and save time for the teacher team because doing so often indicates specific instructional supports that have previously helped the student learn grade-level essential standards.
- **Contributing expertise in evidence-based strategies:** Special educators bring deep knowledge of explicit instruction, scaffolding, and differentiated strategies that strengthen the effectiveness of Tier 2 interventions.
- **Strengthening the system, not separating students:** These educators' role is to support the effectiveness of the overall intervention system. Rather than "owning" certain students, they help teacher teams design supports that allow more students to succeed with grade-level learning.

For this collaboration to function well, the guiding coalition must establish clear expectations for roles and responsibilities. Without that clarity, schools can unintentionally create a culture where struggling students are simply sent to special education teachers, multilingual teachers, or interventionists. Instead, these specialists are partners within a collective system of support that teacher teams design and monitor together.

What is the role of an interventionist in Tier 2 systems?

The interventionist plays a key implementation role in Tier 2 systems, but that role functions best when it is clearly defined as part of a team-based response to student learning needs rather than as a stand-alone program.

Within the guidance of *Taking Action* (Mattos et al., 2025), interventionists typically serve as instructional specialists who deliver targeted instruction aligned to the priorities identified by teacher teams. Their responsibilities often include the following.

- **Delivering targeted Tier 2 instruction:** Interventionists provide additional time and focused instruction for students who have not yet demonstrated proficiency on essential learning targets. This instruction aligns directly with the learning goals identified by teacher teams.
- **Supporting intensive Tier 3 interventions:** In many schools, interventionists also play a central role in providing or coordinating Tier 3 support, which involves more intensive, individualized instruction for students who require additional time and specialized strategies to make progress.
- **Using evidence to guide instruction:** Interventionists monitor student progress through short-cycle assessment and share results with teacher teams so they can adjust instruction and grouping decisions.
- **Partnering with classroom teachers:** Effective interventionists work closely with classroom teachers to ensure Tier 2 support aligns tightly with Tier 1 instruction. This alignment helps students connect intervention learning back to classroom expectations.
- **Helping the system remain responsive:** Because interventionists often support multiple grade levels or teams, they help schools remain flexible by adjusting groups, strategies, and instructional responses as new evidence emerges.

As with other specialized roles, the guiding coalition must clearly define how interventionists fit within the system of support. When expectations are not explicit, interventionists can unintentionally become the place where teachers send struggling students. In a strong Tier 2 system, however, interventionists are part of a coordinated team response, ensuring students receive additional time and targeted instruction while the classroom teacher and team continue to refine core instruction.

Overcoming the Obstacles

Every school wants Tier 2 to work, but the obstacles are real. Not enough staff. Not enough space. Not enough time. And sometimes, not enough clarity about who owns the work. This section looks at those challenges head-on, with practical ways schools can stretch resources, protect time, and share ownership so Tier 2 becomes a reality for every student.

Resources

Many schools face the hard truth that there's not enough staff, space, or materials to offer consistent quality Tier 2 interventions. Whether instructional aides are stretched across too many classrooms or there's a shortage of intervention tools, the options can sometimes look pretty thin.

Building the foundation for the system to work well is critical. Consult *Taking Action* (Mattos et al., 2025) to set up the guiding coalition's actions, the teacher team's actions, and the intervention team's actions in a focused way. There are many staff members who can help with the entire system. The teacher team takes the lead on Tier 2 intervention. Other staff can provide support so the school can assign paraprofessionals during designated intervention blocks. With intentional scheduling, paraprofessionals can provide small-group support or monitor independent practice or extension activities, freeing up certified staff, or those who have the most expertise, to support students who need more time for targeted instruction.

Educators can have a tendency for wanting to purchase programs or curriculum as a solution to Tier 2. We recommend being incredibly cautious about purchasing new resources as a solution to Tier 2 intervention. The solution is to empower teacher teams to plan, design, and deliver Tier 2 intervention on essential standards. However, there can be times when additional resources can support Tier 2 intervention, but it is vital they remain just a resource, not a replacement for instruction.

As teacher teams and guiding coalitions review possible curriculum or digital tools, they must carefully guide teacher teams in using these tools to help students learn essential standards based on assessment evidence. Grant funding can help purchase curriculum or digital tools that align with standards and that teacher teams can use to design Tier 2 intervention and instruction. It is important that schools intentionally select these tools, align them with essential standards and core instruction, and provide scaffolds for students struggling to achieve grade-level essential standards. Additionally, schools may tap into community partnerships for additional relevant learning experiences and support for students needing intervention and extension. Local colleges, nonprofit organizations, or volunteer groups may be able to supply tutors and mentors or even donate materials. Building partnerships not only helps fill resource gaps but also strengthens the connection between schools and their communities.

Finally, consider creative space solutions like temporary dividers, mobile intervention carts, or flexible learning spaces that can make the most of limited square footage. While resource challenges are real, with strategic thinking and collaboration, schools can still create strong Tier 2 systems that serve students well.

A solid Tier 2 plan involves the whole school working together. Principals model support by making intervention a priority and ensuring time is protected. General education teachers work in teams and share ownership of student success, collaborate closely to identify students for Tier 2 intervention, and plan the best next instruction to get there, all while monitoring the practices that are working and which students need something different. Teacher teams also collaborate with intervention teams to ensure aligned support for students who also receive Tier 3 acceleration. Interventionists support the system by offering professional development, coaching, and modeling effective instructional strategies, including small-group instruction. When everyone contributes, Tier 2 becomes not just possible, but powerful.

Time

Scheduling is one of the biggest hurdles when it comes to implementing Tier 2 interventions effectively. Educators often wonder, "When are we supposed to pull students without disrupting Tier 1 instruction? How can we possibly add more to a school day that's already packed?" The challenge is real but not impossible. Just like a well-prepared meal takes planning and the right timing, strong Tier 2 supports require intentional scheduling.

As chapter 6 articulated, the daily schedule must be reworked, and that means exploring creative options to find and reprioritize or repurpose time. Can intervention take place during arrival and dismissal blocks? Is there a separate enrichment period or are there ways to prioritize what students receive outside of essential standards? It's not ideal to eliminate electives or other courses not related to core subjects like English and mathematics, but sometimes this can work. Schools can also build in dedicated intervention periods that don't interfere with core instruction.

Another approach is to embed Tier 2 instruction within the core classroom by differentiating lessons and grouping students based on needs. Teacher teams analyze assessment data to determine which students need Tier 2 intervention; team members may even share students during part of that block so they can collectively respond. Teacher teams would designate, for example, thirty minutes of a ninety-minute block as Tier 2 intervention time and not introduce any new essential standards during that time. That way, students receive targeted help without being pulled from valuable Tier 1 learning time.

Finally, data-driven decision making ensures that time is used wisely. Regular progress monitoring or checks for understanding help staff know when to intensify, adjust, or fade supports. By creatively reimagining time and staying responsive to student needs, schools can make Tier 2 both manageable and meaningful.

Ownership

Students who need Tier 2 support aren't "those kids" or "someone else's job." They are not Tier 2 students. They are students who need additional time and support. They're *our* students. When the whole school takes responsibility, students thrive. When all educators, staff, and administrators embrace responsibility for these students' growth, it creates a culture where every learner is valued and supported. This mindset shifts the focus from isolated interventions to a collective commitment, where success is measured by how well every student progresses.

Shared ownership encourages collaboration among general education teachers, specialists, and support staff. This unified approach ensures consistent interventions and prevents students from falling through the cracks. When teachers collectively monitor progress, share strategies, and communicate openly, Tier 2 students receive timely, targeted support that addresses their unique needs. Collaboration also promotes professional growth, as educators learn from one another and adapt best practices to benefit all learners.

Furthermore, shared ownership fosters a positive environment where students feel seen and understood. It breaks down the isolation that can occur when responsibility is siloed, making it clear that every educator plays a role in each student's success. Students know what essential standard they are focused on during Tier 2 intervention and understand that this additional time and support are not a punishment but a sign that educators believe they will learn with more time and hold that belief as a value. Students' confidence and motivation increase when they know their entire school community supports them and believes they can do it. As a result, engagement increases, academic outcomes improve, and students develop stronger social and emotional skills.

Essentially, promoting shared ownership means acknowledging that Tier 2 students are "all of our kids." When the whole school community invests in their success, students thrive both academically and socially, creating a stronger, more inclusive school culture for all. This collective commitment ensures that no student is overlooked, and every learner not only has the opportunity but also experiences a system designed to ensure they achieve grade-level essential standards, learn at high levels, and reach their full potential.

Using Technology to Enhance Tier 2

Technology has opened powerful new doors for schools working to strengthen Tier 2 instruction. Digital tools can help educators diagnose skill gaps, provide targeted practice, and track student progress more efficiently than ever before. When used well, technology can be the extra set of hands teachers need to make small-group and individualized learning manageable. In addition to early warning systems, artificial intelligence (AI) offers real-time progress monitoring and can help busy teacher teams develop new instructional responses targeted to specific misconceptions in the data. Digital platforms continuously track student growth and engagement, providing instant feedback to teachers.

One major advantage of technology in Tier 2 is the ability to personalize learning. Adaptive programs adjust the level of difficulty in real time, giving students practice that matches their current skill level. Instead of one-size-fits-all worksheets, students receive tasks designed to meet them where they are and move them toward mastery of essential standards.

Data collection is another key benefit. Online assessments, practice platforms, and learning management systems can generate instant feedback and progress reports. Teachers can quickly see which students are improving, which are stuck, and which strategies are working. This reduces the guesswork and makes instructional decisions more precise and timelier.

Technology also makes learning more engaging for students who may already feel discouraged. Interactive games, digital badges, and online lessons can turn practice into something students look forward to. For Tier 2 students who may struggle with confidence, a more engaging format can make a big difference in persistence and motivation.

Collaboration is another area where technology supports Tier 2. Digital platforms allow teachers, interventionists, and specialists to share assessment data, lesson plans, and notes in real time. This creates a stronger alignment across the school and ensures that students get consistent support no matter who is leading the intervention.

At the same time, technology should be used as a support tool, not a replacement for the teacher. No program, platform, or AI tool can replicate the relationship or judgment of a skilled educator. Teachers can interpret the *why* behind the data, provide the encouragement students need, and adjust instruction in ways technology cannot.

AI has gained attention for its ability to generate practice activities, suggest interventions, and analyze data trends. While AI can save teachers time, it is not foolproof. AI tools can make mistakes, misinterpret data, or suggest strategies that don't fit a school's context. Teachers remain the gatekeepers, ensuring that AI-driven suggestions are both accurate and appropriate for their students.

Not all technology is created equal, however. Schools should be careful to choose tools that are research-based, aligned with essential standards, and accessible to all learners. Just because a program is flashy or popular does not mean it will actually strengthen Tier 2 instruction. Intentional selection and ongoing evaluation are critical. Equity is another consideration when integrating technology into Tier 2. Technology can widen gaps if some students don't have reliable access at home or if certain tools don't accommodate diverse learning needs. Schools must ensure that technology-enhanced Tier 2 instruction is inclusive and doesn't unintentionally leave some learners behind.

Ultimately, technology is most powerful in Tier 2 when it amplifies good teaching. It can streamline assessment, free up time for teachers to work directly with students, and create engaging ways to practice essential skills. But it does not replace the teacher's role. With educators leading the way, technology becomes a bridge for more students to cross from struggle to success. Table 7.1 provides some useful dos and don'ts for AI in tiered intervention planning.

Getting the most out of AI depends entirely on the prompt you give it. The clearer and more specific your prompt, the better the results. Be sure to use the exact language from your standards and item specifications to guide the AI in generating accurate and useful responses. Figure 7.1 shows examples of effective prompts you can use to unpack learning targets, build intervention menus, and create aligned assessments.

Table 7.1: Dos and Don'ts for Using AI in Tiered Intervention

Do	Don't
Do use AI to save time on the heavy lifting: Ask AI to help create sample proficiency scales, draft intervention activities, or organize learning targets into logical progressions. **Do use it as a brainstorming partner:** AI can generate multiple approaches to reteach a concept, suggest tiered questioning, or offer differentiated strategies. **Do personalize the outputs:** Always tweak and adjust what AI gives you to match your classroom routines, your student data, and your instructional style. **Do use it to reflect:** AI can help you reframe your language, identify potential misconceptions, or even clean up your lesson reflections.	**Don't blindly copy and paste:** AI doesn't know your pacing, the mathematics program your school uses, or your students' current level of understanding. **Don't skip the data:** AI can't analyze formative assessments for you—you must look at what students know and don't know and use AI to respond. **Don't ignore equity:** AI isn't always inclusive in its examples or materials. Make sure you're reviewing resources to ensure they reflect your classroom community. **Don't forget the human element:** Relationships, team collaboration, real-time feedback, and classroom culture are all key pieces that AI just can't replicate.

Learning Targets and Success Criteria	Unpack this grade 3 ELA Common Core standard RL.3.3. Break it into clear learning targets using student-friendly language. Include the skills students need to master and examples of what success looks like.
	Unpack Algebra 1 standard HAS-REI.B.3. Break it into learning objectives, list prerequisite skills, include skills students need to master, and show examples of what success looks like.
Tier 2 Interventions	Give me Tier 2 intervention strategies for students who are struggling to solve multiplication word problems in grade 3. Focus on equal groups and arrays. Include visuals, manipulatives, and example problems I can use in small-group instruction.
	Create a Tier 2 small-group intervention plan for students in grade 10 who are struggling to identify and analyze theme development in a literary text. Include modeling strategies, guided practice, and activities using short text excerpts for skill building.

Figure 7.1: Example AI prompts for planning tiered intervention.

continued ▶

Extensions	Create extension activities for grade 5 students who already understand how to multiply fractions. Include real-world application tasks, open-ended problems, and opportunities for students to create their own word problems.
	Give me extension-activity ideas for kindergarten students who already identify characters, settings, and events in a story. Include hands-on, creative, or storytelling tasks that deepen comprehension and foster critical thinking.
Assessment Building	Build a grade 3 mathematics assessment aligned to CCSS.Math-Content.3.OA.A.3 with at least four question types: multiple choice that has more than one correct answer, short constructed response, a multistep word problem, and a real-world performance task using multiplication and division within one hundred.
	Create a high school ELA assessment aligned to CCSS.ELA-Literacy.RI.9–10.8. Include a nonfiction text and questions that require students to analyze argument structure. Use a mix of multiple choice and short answer, plus an extended response that asks for evaluation of reasoning and evidence.
	Create a grade 1 ELA assessment aligned to CCSS.ELA-Literacy.RL.1.2. Include a short grade-level passage (level 8–10) and a mix of question types: multiple choice to assess key details, a short-answer question to describe characters and setting, and a drawing or labeling activity to show understanding of the story's events.

Source for standard: NGA & CCSSO, 2010a, 2010b.

Working Together to Support Students

Strong Tier 2 support is built on collaboration and clear roles for three teams: the guiding coalition, the teacher team, and the intervention team. It's not the responsibility of one teacher or one role: It takes everyone. When all people in a school work together on a specific goal, no one feels overwhelmed, and students get the consistent, targeted support they need to grow.

Start by clearly defining roles. The teacher team is responsible for leading Tier 2 intervention. The lead interventionist can deliver small-group instruction in Tier 2 as the schedule allows and often is the lead on foundational skills support in Tier 3 time, depending on the structure of the schedule and the people involved. The intervention team leads Tier 3 systems and ensures students are receiving support on foundational skills. The intervention team also monitors the impact of that support both on the foundational skills and on students' ability to grow and transfer those skills into core instruction. Thus, when Tier 3 is working well, students will see growth in their grade-level essential standards. Both an interventionist and the teacher team must track student progress on essential standards and any foundational skill in Tier 3. We don't want students to do well in Tier 3 support but not be able to transfer that in different settings, so watching that data is incredibly important. General education teachers, in teacher teams, contribute classroom data, share insights about student strengths and challenges, and help align Tier 2 strategies with additional support on grade-level essential standards.

The guiding coalition, including administrators, ensures the team has dedicated time to meet, plan, and follow through on interventions. The guiding coalition monitors the effectiveness of Tier 2 systems across the school. When Tier 2 systems are working well, fewer students will need Tier 2 support and more students receiving Tier 3 support will show growth. The guiding coalition helps develop roles for all involved. For example, support staff may be able to assist with things like monitoring behavior, collecting data, or helping students transition smoothly.

It's also important to make sure every team member is prepared. Educators need regular training on how to identify essential standards, work with learning targets, execute high-quality instruction, lead small groups, monitor progress effectively, and use evidence-based materials. Teams should also have time built into their schedules to plan, talk through what's working, and adjust instruction as needed. When schools prioritize this kind of shared effort, Tier 2 becomes more focused, more responsive, and more effective for the students who need it most.

Maximizing Impact

Making Tier 2 support truly effective requires ongoing attention, reflection, and responsiveness. It's not enough to put an intervention in place and hope it works. Schools must regularly evaluate how teachers deliver interventions and whether they're making a difference. The guiding coalition leads reviewing progress-monitoring data, checking for fidelity to the intervention plan, and discussing student outcomes as a team. If students aren't making progress, it's important to ask why and be willing to adjust. Sometimes the area requiring adjustment is the frequency or duration of support, sometimes it's the instructional strategy, and other times it's about matching the right support to the right student need.

Celebrating growth is equally important. Progress might be small at first, but acknowledging it builds momentum. Recognizing even modest improvements helps students feel successful and encourages them to stay engaged in the learning process. It also reminds educators and families that the effort is working. This intentional reflection on and celebration of the concrete actions that lead to results build teacher collective efficacy and student efficacy.

Finally, it's important to look at the whole student. Academic growth doesn't happen in isolation. Combining academic interventions with behavior and social-emotional support ensures students get what they need to succeed not only in the classroom but also in how they feel, relate to others, and navigate challenges. A thoughtful, layered approach helps Tier 2 have the greatest possible impact on student success.

Accessing Additional Instructional Resources and Materials to Support Tier 2

While many instructional curricula embed support for intervention and extension, the process of curating additional high-quality resources can often be time consuming and overwhelming for educators. Having access to a broader range of supplemental materials not only enhances instructional flexibility but also streamlines the planning process across multiple tiers of support. Although the resources shown in figure 7.2 are particularly well suited for Tier 2 intervention, you can also effectively integrate them into Tier 1 instruction to reinforce foundational skills, differentiate learning, and extend student understanding. Expanding access to these tools allows you to respond more efficiently to diverse student needs while maintaining instructional rigor and alignment to essential standards.

ELA Resources	
CommonLit	www.commonlit.org/en/home This free digital library of leveled reading passages has built-in assessments and tools, making it an excellent resource for planning interventions in reading comprehension.
Florida Center for Reading Research	https://fcrr.org/resources This resource provides printable, research-based small-group phonics activities for grades K–5.
Flyleaf Online Decodables	https://flyleafpublishing.com This resource provides online access to high-quality decodable text to support literacy development at school and at home.
MagicSchool AI	https://app.magicschool.ai/tools With this resource, you can streamline planning for interventions and extensions by generating customized instructional resources quickly and efficiently.

ReadWorks	www.readworks.org This resource gives you access to high-quality reading passages that support the development of fluency and reading comprehension.
University of Florida Literacy Institute Foundations Toolbox	https://ufli.education.ufl.edu/foundations/toolbox This resource is designed to build students' alphabet knowledge and decoding and encoding skills.
Mathematics Resources	
The Curriculum Corner	www.thecurriculumcorner.com In this resource, you'll find hands-on math practice sets, small-group games, and skill-based math for students K–6.
The Math Learning Center	www.mathlearningcenter.org/apps This resource provides digital number lines, ten frames, base 10 blocks, and fractions for visual models.
NRICH	https://nrich.maths.org/students This resource gives you access to visual logic puzzles, hands-on problem-solving tasks, and strategic games.
Tang Math	https://tangmath.com Here, you'll find hands-on number puzzles and games that build number flexibility and fluency.

Figure 7.2: Online resources to support Tier 2 instruction.

Are You Ready?

Putting Tier 2 interventions into practice is similar to serving up a second helping in a busy kitchen. It requires planning, teamwork, and flexibility. When resources are tight and time is short, schools need to work together and make the most of every tool and partnership they have.

When you build strong Tier 2 systems, you do more than help students who need extra time and support. You show that every child deserves a real chance to succeed. The second helping really does matter. By being resourceful, working together, using data, and making smart use of tools like AI, Tier 2 becomes more than just a backup plan. It turns into a balanced meal that gives students what they need to grow, gain confidence, and achieve their goals.

After your team has assessed your readiness, use the reflection questions in the reproducible tool "Pause and Take Action: Chapter 7" to determine the next steps to build your Tier 2 intervention system.

Throughout this book, you have examined the mindsets, leadership, schedules, and practical steps needed to ensure students get the time and support they need. Turning ideas into action is not always easy, but it can happen when schools work together and act with purpose. As you read the epilogue, take a moment to reflect on the deeper reasons for this work and how a strong Tier 2 system can shape your school's culture and your students' futures.

Pause and Take Action: Chapter 7

Consider the following questions to determine how your teacher team will tackle challenges.

- What are a few of our biggest obstacles in implementing a Tier 2 system of support that is not overwhelming?
- What are our biggest assets in addressing these obstacles? How might we develop a concrete solution to pilot and notice the changes in student learning and the adult workflow?
- Which questions are most prevalent in our school and our work in building a Tier 2 system? Which solutions resonate? How might these solutions help us create our own solution to implement and notice its impact on student learning and each team's workflow?
- How do we handle the issue of time? What might be causing our challenges with time? Is there anything we can stop doing to create time for more targeted and effective Tier 2 support?
- Do we have the three teams (guiding coalition, teacher teams, intervention team) in place? Do members of those teams understand their role in a strong Tier 2 system? What conversations and changes need to take place to strengthen each team's actions to ensure a system that works?
- How do we currently utilize AI? Do our teams need support in us ng AI in intentional ways? What might that look like?
- How do our teams use programs and curriculum in Tier 2 intervention? Is it a replacement for intervention or do we use it intentionally to support teacher teams in developing focused, targeted Tier 2 intervention strategies based on the assessment evidence measuring essential standards?

Team Action Steps

Now that you've reflected, identify two strengths of your Tier 2 systems you want to intentionally keep doing.

Identify two steps your teacher teams will take to strengthen your Tier 2 work and when those steps will occur.

Second Helpings © 2027 Solution Tree Press • SolutionTree.com
Visit **go.SolutionTree.com/RTIatWork** to download this free reproducible.

Epilogue

The second helpings food metaphor is fun, but the message behind it is deeply serious. By this point, it should be clear that Tier 2 is not simply another program or optional layer of support in schools. It is a vital part of a school's promise to ensure every student receives the time and support needed to learn at high levels. From assessments as the appetizer to planning, instruction, student ownership, learning dispositions, schedules, and creative problem solving, each chapter has added an essential ingredient. Together, they show that Tier 2 isn't just an extra help for a few students. It is a shared commitment to respond when students need more.

In the introduction, we invited you to picture a table surrounded by people you care about, a well-prepared meal, and the satisfaction of a second helping. That image still matters here at the end. In effective schools, Tier 1 is the strong first serving—carefully designed, high quality, and intended for every learner. Tier 2 is the second helping—timely, intentional, and responsive to what a student needs to fully thrive. It is not a replacement for core instruction, not a separate track, and not a signal that a student has failed. It is a proactive and systemic response that says, "We noticed what you need, and we will respond."

That kind of response does not happen by accident. It requires the guiding coalition to set priorities and protect time. It requires teacher teams that clarify essential standards and analyze evidence of learning to plan Tier 2 intervention for all students who need more time on those grade-level essential standards. It requires an intervention team that coordinates and provides support when students need time to learn foundational skills beyond Tier 1 and Tier 2 support. It requires schools to reject the idea that struggling students belong to someone else. Tier 2 works only when adults embrace collective responsibility and design structures that make support timely, focused, and doable.

That is why Tier 2 cannot become a replacement for core instruction, a loose collection of interventions, a referral pathway, or a place where students are sent. It must be intentionally planned as a regular, protected, and essential part of a school's daily work. When schools build Tier 2 systems this way, they create more than intervention blocks and schedules. They create belonging. They create access. They create a culture where students experience support not as punishment but as a promise. Technology, resources, and strategies can help, but they don't replace the heart of the Tier 2 system—which is you! As we close this book, we want you to walk away with this key idea: As you move forward, keep refining the recipes. Keep setting the table. Keep using evidence to decide what students need and keep building and refining systems that ensure they receive it. Stay committed to the idea that with the right support, at the right time, every student can grow, achieve, and move forward with confidence. The real promise of second helpings in schools means no student is overlooked, no need is ignored, and no learner is left to navigate their struggle alone. As you move forward, keep students' needs met, conversations active, and your belief strong. Every student deserves a seat at this table, strong instruction, timely support, and adults who refuse to give up on their success. Your dedication makes sure no one leaves wanting more from their learning.

References and Resources

Ainsworth, L. (2003). *Power standards: Identifying the standards that matter the most.* Advanced Learning Press.

Alkharusi, H. (2013). Canonical correlational models of students' perceptions of assessment tasks, motivational orientations, and learning strategies. *International Journal of Instruction, 6*(1), 21–38.

Allensworth, E., Correa, M., & Ponisciak, S. (2008). *From high school to the future: ACT preparation—Too much, too late.* Consortium on Chicago School Research.

Almarzouki, A. F. (2024). Stress, working memory, and academic performance: A neuroscience perspective. *Stress, 27*(1). https://doi.org/10.1080/10253890.2024.2364333

Andrade, H. L., Bennett, R. E., & Cizek, G. J. (Eds.). (2019). *Handbook of formative assessment in the disciplines.* Routledge.

Andrade, H. L., & Brookhart, S. M. (2020). Classroom assessment as the co-regulation of learning. *Assessment in Education: Principles, Policy and Practice, 27*(4), 350–372.

Andrade, H. L., & Cizek, G. J. (Eds.). (2010). *Handbook of formative assessment.* Routledge.

Bandura, A. (1997). *Self-efficacy: The exercise of control.* Freeman.

Barbayannis, G., Bandari, M., Zheng, X., Baquerizo, H., Pecor, K. W., & Ming, X. (2022). Academic stress and mental well-being in college students: Correlations, affected groups, and COVID-19. *Frontiers in Psychology, 13.* https://doi.org/10.3389/fpsyg.2022.886344

Bloom, B. S. (Ed.). (1956). *Taxonomy of educational objectives: The classification of educational goals—Handbook I: Cognitive domain.* McKay.

Boudett, K. P., City, E. A., & Murnane, R. J. (Eds.). (2013). *Data wise: A step-by-step guide to using assessment results to improve teaching and learning* (Rev. and expanded ed.). Harvard Education Press.

Brookhart, S. M., & McMillan, J. H. (Eds.). (2020). *Classroom assessment and educational measurement*. Routledge.

Brookhart, S. M., McTighe, J., Stiggins, R., & Wiliam, D. (2019). *The future of assessment practices: Comprehensive and balanced assessment systems*. Learning Sciences International. Accessed at https://cdn.prod.website-files.com/5b97ca09a5d9b67fc13c7667/670590 7ee728eb553204d105_The-Future-of-Assessment-A-Comprehensive-Assessment-Systems -LSI-Paper-.pdf on October 20, 2025.

Buffum, A., & Mattos, M. (Eds.). (2015). *It's about time: Planning interventions and extensions in elementary school*. Solution Tree Press.

Calderón, M. (2011). *Teaching Reading & Comprehension to English Learners, K-5*. Solution Tree Press.

Circles. (2023). *Q1 2024 trends: Workplace insights and trends in work-life balance, employee well-being and social connection*. Author.

Dimich, N. (2009). Finding meaning in numbers. In T. R. Guskey (Ed.), *The principal as assessment leader* (pp. 149–173). Solution Tree Press.

Dimich, N. (2024). *Design in five: Essential phases to create engaging assessment practice* (2nd ed.). Solution Tree Press.

Dimich, N., & Baker-Busby, A. (2026). *The handbook for design in five: Assessment tools and protocols for teachers and teams*. Solution Tree Press.

Duckworth, A. (2016). *Grit: The power of passion and perseverance*. Scribner.

DuFour, R., DuFour, R., Eaker, R., Many, T. W., Mattos, M., & Muhammad, A. (2024). *Learning by doing: A handbook for Professional Learning Communities at Work* (4th ed.). Solution Tree Press.

Dweck, C. S. (2015). *Mindset: Changing the way you think to fulfil your potential* (Updated ed.). Random House.

Dysarz, K. (2018a, April). *Checking in: Are math assignments measuring up?* EdTrust. Accessed at https://edtrust.org/wp-content/uploads/2014/09/CheckingIn_MATH-ANALYSIS _FINAL_5.pdf on October 20, 2025.

Dysarz, K. (2018b, April 3). *The power of classroom assignments* [Blog post]. EdTrust. Accessed at https://edtrust.org/blog/power-classroom-assignments on October 20, 2025.

EdTrust. (2022, October 5). *Improving rigor & representation in P–12 curriculum*. Accessed at https://edtrust.org/rti/improving-rigor-representation-in-p-12-curriculum on October 20, 2025.

EdTrust. (2024, December). *Federal policy guide to improve equity in state summative assessments*. Author. Accessed at https://edtrust.org/wp-content/uploads/2024/11 /Assessment-Innovations-Summary-FED-V4.pdf on October 20, 2025.

Fisher, D., & Frey, N. (2014). *Checking for understanding: Formative assessment techniques for your classroom* (2nd ed.). ASCD.

Florida Center for Reading Research. (n.d.). *Resources*. Accessed at https://fcrr.org/resources on October 23, 2025.

Forage. (2023, June 2). *What are collaboration skills? Definition and examples* [Blog post]. Accessed at www.theforage.com/blog/skills/collaboration-skills on October 21, 2025.

Fuchs, D., & Fuchs, L. S. (2006). Introduction to response to intervention: What, why, and how valid is it? *Reading Research Quarterly*, *41*(1), 93–99. https://doi.org/10.1598/RRQ.41.1.4

Gaumer Erickson, A. S., & Noonan, P. M. (2022). *Teaching self-regulation: Seventy-five instructional activities to foster independent, proactive students, grades 6–12*. Solution Tree Press.

Gobena, G. A. (2024). Effects of academic stress on students' academic achievements and its implications for their future lives. *Anatolian Journal of Education*, *9*(1), 113-130.

Goddard, R. D., Hoy, W. K., & Hoy, A. W. (2000). Collective teacher efficacy: Its meaning, measure, and impact on student achievement. *American Educational Research Journal*, *37*(2), 479–507.

Goddard, R. D., Hoy, W. K., & Hoy, A. W. (2004). Collective efficacy beliefs: Theoretical developments, empirical evidence, and future directions. *Educational Researcher*, *33*(3), 3–13.

Goodwin, B., & Rouleau, K. (2022). *The new classroom instruction that works: The best research-based strategies for increasing student achievement*. ASCD.

Guskey, T. R. (Ed.). (2009). *The principal as assessment leader*. Solution Tree Press.

Guskey, T. R. (2015). Mastery learning. In J. D. Wright (Ed.), *International encyclopedia of the social and behavioral sciences* (2nd ed., pp. 752–759). Elsevier.

Hamilton, L., Halverson, R., Jackson, S. S., Mandinach, E., Supovitz, J. A., & Wayman, J. C. (2009). *Using student achievement data to support instructional decision making*. National Center for Education Evaluation and Regional Assistance. Accessed at https://repository.upenn.edu/server/api/core/bitstreams/72507cc0-726c-477a-acf4-8a519d2836eb/content on October 21, 2025.

Hamilton, L., Kaufman, J., and Diliberti, M. (2020). *Teaching and Leading Through a Pandemic: Key Findings from the American Educator Panels Spring 2020 COVID-19 Surveys*. Santa Monica, CA: RAND Corporation. Accessed at www.rand.org/pubs/research_reports/RRA168-2.html on April 22, 2026.

Hannigan, J. D., & Hannigan, J. (2024). *Behavior academies: Targeted interventions that work!* Solution Tree Press.

Hannigan, J., Hannigan, J. D., Mattos, M., & Buffum, A. (2021). *Behavior solutions: Teaching academic and social skills through RTI at Work*. Solution Tree Press.

Hattie, J. (2023). *Visible learning: The sequel—A synthesis of over 2,100 meta-analyses relating to achievement*. Routledge.

Heissel, J. A., Adam, E. K., Doleac, J. L., Figlio, D. N., & Meer, J. (2021). Testing, stress, and performance: How students respond physiologically to high-stakes testing. *Education Finance and Policy, 16*(2), 183–208.

Hess, K. (2018). *A local assessment toolkit to promote deeper learning: Transforming research into practice*. Corwin.

Jones, S. M., Brush, K. E., Wettje, S., Ramirez, T., Poddar, A., Kannarr, A., et al. (2022, November). *Navigating SEL from the inside out: Looking inside and across leading SEL programs—A practical resource for schools and OST providers*. Harvard Graduate School of Education. Accessed at https://wallacefoundation.org/sites/default/files/2024-10/navigating-social-and-emotional-learning-from-the-inside-out-middle-high-school.doi_.10.59656%252FYD-OS7616.001.pdf on October 21, 2025.

Kramer, S. V. (Ed.). (2021). *Charting the course for leaders: Lessons from priority schools in a PLC at Work*. Solution Tree Press.

Kramer, S. V., Sonju, B., Mattos, M., & Buffum, A. (2021). *Best practices at Tier 2: Supplemental interventions for additional student support, elementary*. Solution Tee Press.

Ladson-Billings, G. (2021a). I'm here for the hard re-set: Post pandemic pedagogy to preserve our culture. *Equity and Excellence in Education, 54*(1), 68–78. https://doi.org/10.1080/10665684.2020.1863883

Ladson-Billings, G. (2021b). Three decades of culturally relevant, responsive, & sustaining pedagogy: What lies ahead? *The Educational Forum, 85*(4), 351–354. https://doi.org/10.1080/00131725.2021.1957632

Lapp, D. K., Wolsey, T. D., Wood, K. D., & Johnson, K. (2014). *Mining complex text, grades 6–12: Using and creating graphic organizers to grasp content and share new understandings*. Corwin.

Leighton, J. P. (2020). Cognitive diagnosis is not enough: The challenge of measuring learning with classroom assessments. In S. M. Brookhart & J. H. McMillan (Eds.), *Classroom assessment and educational measurement* (pp. 27–45). Routledge.

Levitan, S., & Munyan-Penney, N. (2024a, April). *Making assessment reports more meaningful for students & families*. EdTrust. Accessed at https://edtrust.org/wp-content/uploads/2014/09/Assessments-Reporting-V10.pdf on October 20, 2025.

Levitan, S., & Munyan-Penney, N. (2024b, February). *Advocates' guide to demanding racially & culturally inclusive state assessments*. EdTrust. Accessed at https://edtrust.org/wp-content/uploads/2014/09/Inclusive-Assessments-Final.pdf on October 20, 2025.

Levy, F., & Murnane, R. J. (2004). *The new division of labor: How computers are creating the next job market*. Princeton University Press.

Maeker, P., & Heller, J. (2023). *Literacy in a PLC at Work: Guiding teams to get going and get better in grades K–6 reading*. Solution Tree Press.

Mansell, K. E., & Kirksey, J. J. (2025). *Exploring the effectiveness of the PLC at Work process in Texas schools* (Report). Center for Innovative Research in Change, Leadership, and Education, Texas Tech University.

Many, T. W., Maffoni, M. J., Sparks, S. K., & Thomas, T. F. (2022). *Energize your teams: Powerful tools for coaching collaborative teams in PLCs at Work*. Solution Tree Press.

Marques, S. C., Gallagher, M. W., & Lopez, S. J. (2017). Hope- and academic-related outcomes: A meta-analysis. *School Mental Health: A Multidisciplinary Research and Practice Journal, 9*(3), 250–262. https://doi.org/10.1007/s12310-017-9212-9

Marques, S. C., Lopez, S. J., & Mitchell, J. (2013). The role of hope, spirituality and religious practice in adolescents' life satisfaction: Longitudinal findings. *Journal of Happiness Studies: An Interdisciplinary Forum on Subjective Well-Being, 14*(1), 251–261. https://doi.org/10.1007/s10902-012-9329-3

Marzano, R. J. (2007). *The art and science of teaching: A comprehensive framework for effective instruction*. ASCD.

Marzano, R. J. (2009). *Designing and teaching learning goals and objectives*. Marzano Resources.

Marzano, R. J. (2017). *The new art and science of teaching*. Solution Tree Press.

Marzano, R. J. (2019). *The handbook for the new art and science of teaching*. Solution Tree Press.

Marzano, R. J., Pickering, D. J., & Pollock, J. E. (2001). *Classroom instruction that works: Research-based strategies for increasing student achievement*. ASCD.

The Math Learning Center. (n.d.). *Math apps*. Accessed at www.mathlearningcenter.org/apps on October 23, 2025.

Mattos, M., & Buffum, A. (Eds.). (2015). *It's about time: Planning interventions and extensions in secondary school*. Solution Tree Press.

Mattos, M., Buffum, A., Malone, J., Cruz, L. F., Dimich, N., & Schuhl, S. (2025). *Taking action: A handbook for RTI at Work* (2nd ed.). Solution Tree Press.

Meckler, L., & Natanson, H. (2024, January 18). White House urges schools to address absenteeism amid troubling data. *The Washington Post*. Accessed at www.washingtonpost.com/education/2024/01/18/school-attendance-absenteeism-biden on October 21, 2025.

Michigan Association of Intermediate School Administrators General Education Leadership Network Early Literacy Task Force (2023). *Essential instructional practices in early literacy: K to 3*. Lansing, MI: Authors. Accessed at www.gomaisa.org/downloads/gelndocs/k-3_literacy_essentials.pdf on April 20, 2026.

Mind the Graph. (2024, February 28). *From paper to practice: Intended and enacted curriculum*. LinkedIn. Accessed at www.linkedin.com/pulse/from-paper-practice-intended-enacted-curriculum-mind-the-graph-s6dmf on October 21, 2025.

Munyan-Penney, N., & Mehrotra, S. (2023, April). *Future of assessments: Centering equity and the lived experiences of students, families, and educators*. EdTrust. Accessed at https://edtrust.org/wp-content/uploads/2014/09/Future_Assessments_FINAL.pdf on October 20, 2025.

National Center on Intensive Intervention. (2016). *Principles for designing intervention in mathematics*. Office of Special Education, U.S. Department of Education. Accessed at https://intensiveintervention.org/sites/default/files/Princip_Effect_Math_508.pdf on April 3, 2026.

National Governors Association Center for Best Practices & Council of Chief State School Officers. (2010a). *Common Core State Standards for English language arts and literacy in history/social studies, science, and technical subjects*. Authors. Accessed at https://corestandards.org/wp-content/uploads/2023/09/ELA_Standards1.pdf on October 22, 2025.

National Governors Association Center for Best Practices & Council of Chief State School Officers. (2010b). *Common Core State Standards for mathematics*. Authors. Accessed at https://corestandards.org/wp-content/uploads/2023/09/Math_Standards1.pdf on October 22, 2025.

National School Reform Faculty. (n.d.). *Exactly what is Critical Friends Group work?* Harmony Education Center. Accessed at https://nsrfharmony.org/whatiscfgwork/ on April 24, 2024.

The Nation's Report Card. (n.d.). *Achievement gaps dashboard*. Accessed at www.nationsreportcard.gov/dashboards/achievement_gaps.aspx on June 9, 2016.

NGSS Lead States. (2013). Next Generation Science Standards: For states, by states. The National Academies Press.

Ng, V., Koh, D., & Chia, S. E. (2003). Examination stress, salivary cortisol, and academic performance. *Psychological reports*, *93*(3 Pt 2), 1133–1134. https://doi.org/10.2466/pr0.2003.93.3f.1133

NRICH. (n.d.). *Students*. Accessed at https://nrich.maths.org/students on October 23, 2025.

Pearson, P. D., & Gallagher, M. C. (1983). The instruction of reading comprehension. *Contemporary Educational Psychology*, *8*(3), 317–344.

Pérez-Jorge, D., Boutaba-Alehyan, M., González-Contreras, A. I., & Pérez-Pérez, I. (2025). Examining the effects of academic stress on student well-being in higher education. *Humanities and Social Sciences Communications*, *12*, 449.

Reeves, D. (Ed.). (2007). *Ahead of the curve: The power of assessment to transform teaching and learning*. Solution Tree Press.

Ritchhart, R., Church, M., & Morrison, K. (2011). *Making thinking visible: How to promote engagement, understanding, and independence for all learners*. Jossey-Bass.

Roberts, M. (2019). *Enriching the learning: Meaningful extensions for proficient students in a PLC at Work*. Solution Tree Press.

Rosenshine, B. (2012). Principles of instruction: Research-based strategies that all teachers should know. *American Educator*, *36*(1), 12–19, 39.

Ruiz-Primo, M. A., & Brookhart, S. M. (2018). *Using feedback to improve learning*. Routledge.

Sadler, D. R. (1989). Formative assessment and the design of instructional systems. *Instructional Science, 18*(2), 119–144.

Saunders, E. (2023). *Stick the learning: Brain-based teaching techniques to increase retention, application, and transfer*. Solution Tree Press.

Schmoker, M. (2018). *Focus: Elevating the essentials to radically improve student learning* (2nd ed.). ASCD.

Schuhl, S., Toncheff, M., Deinhart, J., & Buckhalter, B. (2025). *Mathematics strategies for Tier 1 and Tier 2 interventions in a PLC at Work*. Solution Tree Press.

Skaalvik, E. M., & Skaalvik, S. (2007). Dimensions of teacher self-efficacy and relations with strain factors, perceived collective teacher efficacy, and teacher burnout. *Journal of Educational Psychology, 99*(3), 611–625. https://doi.org/10.1037/0022-0663.99.3.611

TNTP. (2023). *The opportunity myth: What students can show us about how school is letting them down—And how to fix it.* Accessed at https://tntp.org/publication/the-opportunity-myth on April 1, 2026.

Tomlinson, C. A. (2014). *The differentiated classroom: Responding to the needs of all learners* (2nd ed.). ASCD.

Tschannen-Moran, M. (2001). Collaboration and the need for trust. *Journal of Educational Administration, 39*(4), 308–331.

University of Florida Literacy Institute. (n.d.). *UFLI foundations toolbox*. Accessed at https://ufli.education.ufl.edu/foundations/toolbox on October 23, 2025.

Webb, J. (2021). *The metacognition handbook: A practical guide for teachers and school leaders.* John Catt Educational.

Webb, N. L. (1997). *Criteria for alignment of expectations and assessments in mathematics and science education (Research monograph no. 6)*. National Institute for Science Education. Accessed at https://files.eric.ed.gov/fulltext/ED414305.pdf on October 22, 2025.

Wiliam, D. (2010). An integrative summary of the research literature and implications for a new theory of formative assessment. In H. L. Andrade & G. J. Cizek (Eds.), *Handbook of formative assessment* (pp. 18–40). Routledge.

Wiliam, D., & Leahy, S. (2024). *Embedding formative assessment: Practical techniques for K–12 classrooms*. Solution Tree Press.

Willis, J., Arnold, J., & DeLuca, C. (2023). Accessibility in assessment for learning: Sharing criteria for success. *Frontiers in Education, 8*. https://doi.org/10.3389/feduc.2023.1170454

Wright, J. D. (Ed.). (2015). *International encyclopedia of the social and behavioral sciences* (2nd ed.). Elsevier.

Index

Taking Action
Mike Mattos, Austin Buffum, Janet Malone, Luis F. Cruz, Nicole Dimich, and Sarah Schuhl
The second edition of the bestseller *Taking Action* delves deeper into the essential actions needed to create a highly effective multitiered system of supports. New recommendations and tools are included to better target assessments, engage students, and proactively address resistance.
BKG136

Design in Five
Nicole Dimich
This second edition of the best-selling *Design in Five* is the book you need to design and use assessment well. It offers new and targeted information for reimagining assessment practices, as well as refined processes and protocols to fully engage learners.
BKG167

The Big Book of Tools for RTI at Work
William M. Ferriter, Mike Mattos, and Rob J. Meyer
Discover a robust set of tools for teachers and leaders to employ on their journey to implementing effective additional support for struggling students. Practical and full of resources, this book supplies educators with the means to transform their school response to intervention process.
BKG132

Best Practices at Tier 2 [Elementary & Secondary]
Bob Sonju, Sharon V. Kramer, Mike Mattos, and Austin Buffum
Whether you're working with RTI or multitiered system of supports (MTSS), the RTI at Work™ process has you covered. With the guidance of this essential series, you'll have the tools and strategies you need to implement a collaborative system of supports that nurtures behavioral and academic success for every student.
BKF714, BKF715

Solution Tree | Press — a division of Solution Tree

Visit SolutionTree.com or call 800.733.6786 to order.

We don't just help schools make a change, we help them ***be* the change**

REAL IMPACT. RELEVANT SOLUTIONS. RESULTS-DRIVEN APPROACH.

From funding to faculty retention, the evolving demands schools face can be overwhelming. That's where we come in. With professional development rooted in decades of research and delivered by many of the educators who literally wrote the book on it, we empower schools to achieve meaningful change with real, sustainable results.

The change starts here. We can make it happen together.

See how we can get real results for your school or district.

Scan the code or visit:

SolutionTree.com/Results-Driven

WE CAN!

Solution Tree

LET'S SEE WHAT **WE CAN** DO TOGETHE